I0080061

Whatever Is

EIGHT SACRED QUALITIES

TO RENEW YOUR

MIND AND TRANSFORM

YOUR LIFE

MADYSON RAY

ILLUMIFY
MEDIA.COM

Whatever Is

Published by
Illumify Media Global
www.IllumifyMedia.com
"Let's bring your book to life!"

Library of Congress Control Number: 2025907195
Paperback ISBN: 978-1-964251-64-6

Cover design by Debbie Lewis

Printed in the United States of America

Contents

Preface

Lord,

I thank You for giving me the vision to write this book. Thank You for the resources You have provided me, including a laptop, the Bible, and a great support system. Thank You for reassuring me that what I'm about to write about is what You want me to write. Thank You for filling me with peace even when I doubt my writing abilities. Thank You for also filling me with the Holy Spirit, so my wisdom is not from me but from You. As I write this book, I pray that it's not my words but Yours. I want You to be glorified throughout this process—direct my thoughts, Father, to be centered on You. I've asked You to use me over and over again, so please let this book be a blessing to Your children. I know Your Word is truth, and we are getting further and further away from the truth in this world. Help me to point back to it with every word I write. You are an excellent, good Father who will never lead me astray. Like a shepherd leads their sheep, Father God, please guide me. All glory to You forever and ever, Amen.

You guys, God is so good and faithful. I would never have thought I would be here writing this book, but wow, here I am. Let me tell you why I have decided to write. When I started writing this book, I was a junior in college and attended a small NAIA (National Association of Intercollegiate Athletics) school. As a junior in high school, I was recruited to run track at Midland University. This school is only thirty minutes from my hometown, Blair, Nebraska, so I was initially a little unsure. However, I visited the school and liked all it had to offer. And fun fact: it was the only school I ever visited. I had a couple of meetings with the track coach and got excited about being an athlete in college. I committed and signed a letter of intent. Honestly, I wasn't the best athlete, and I had earned another scholarship for leadership, so I wouldn't even be going to school on an athletic scholarship, but I won't bore you with all the details. I ended up going to Midland University. I started majoring in education because *my* plan was to be a kindergarten teacher and eventually a principal. I'd had that plan since I was a little kindergartener and dressed like a principal for Halloween. Anyway, I also started off running on the track team, and I got involved in just about everything a student could get involved in. It was great!

I had been running track since seventh grade, and when I got to high school, my only events were the 100-meter hurdles and the 300-meter hurdles. I loved it because it was challenging, but my mom was always scared to watch me. So when I got to college, guess what I did? Hurdles! But I was always striving for something more. I wanted to be challenged. I figured out that the pentathlon and heptathlon were two events I could participate in. The pentathlon includes all of the following: 60-meter hurdles, long jump, high jump, shot put, and 800-meter run. With the heptathlon, the 60-meter hurdles turn into 100-meter hurdles, and they add the javelin and the 200-meter dash. To my surprise, my coach let me start training for it! So, I learned four new events during the indoor season and two more as we moved outdoors. I loved it. There were frustrating moments, moments of celebration and small triumphs, and moments of defeat. But through that process, I learned to give myself grace and not take myself so seriously because I was learning these things for the first time.

In the end, I completed my whole first year in numerous meets. I would run hurdles, sprint, and jump and was having fun. I was even so motivated to improve that I practiced with my coach the following summer. However, I was having a hard time breathing and could never fully catch my breath. It had been happening during the previous season, but now it was getting worse, and I knew it wasn't because I was out of shape. I went to the doctor, and they did some tests. I dislike going to the doctor. Getting blood drawn is the worst. But I was desperate to find answers and get better so I could continue my track career without difficulty. I visited many doctors, and they concluded that I had sports-induced asthma and vocal cord dysfunction. So, in non-doctor terms, asthma makes it hard to breathe out, and VCD makes it hard to breathe in. If you can imagine breathing through a straw, that is what it's comparable to. I was devastated because I was so determined to make new personal records. They didn't tell me I had to stop doing track, but this new diagnosis made running much more difficult. I sat out at the beginning of my sophomore year but eventually was able to participate again.

Along with all these breathing problems, I felt like I was being bullied by one of the other athletes. She would start drama with me for no reason and accuse me of saying things about her that I would never say about anyone. My breathing, however, was getting to the point where I could not finish workouts. I dreaded going to practice every day, knowing I would be unable to breathe and about to pass out. I also dreaded being looked down upon by one of my teammates, who I knew was talking about me behind my back. I was debating whether I should just step away from the track team. I practiced hurdles a week before going home for Christmas and doing the best I had ever done at practice. My form was excellent, and my coach was impressed. On one of the run-throughs, though, I hit a hurdle with my ankle so hard that the entire hurdle fell over. I could not walk and had to sit out of practice for the rest of the week. I felt ridiculous. People hit hurdles all the time! However, I still have a bump on my ankle to this day, so it must have been some kind of serious injury. Then we went home for Christmas break. I continued to do some at-home workouts while I was away from school, and I even went back to Midland a few times for practices, even though my foot was black-and-blue.

We all returned to school at the end of January, but Midland was trying to prevent the spread of COVID, so we all had to test before entering our dorms. I felt fine and wasn't worried about the test, but guess what? It was *positive*, and I was pissed. I loved school, and this was a setback. After bawling in my car for an hour, I went back home and lay in my bed, depressed. The next day, I had a lot of trouble breathing. I couldn't even walk upstairs without gasping for air. I knew that God was directing me to step away from the team. With one thing after another, He was trying to catch my attention. And this time, He finally did.

I returned to Midland, gave my coaches a thank-you letter for all they had done for me. It was the hardest decision of my life. I didn't know what to do with my spare time. I felt lonely. Track was a part of me, and when I stopped doing it, I felt like I didn't know myself.

We had a service at church one week after I'd made that heartbreaking decision. My church believes in the gifts of the Spirit, like prophesying, speaking in tongues, healing, etc. My pastor is fantastic, and you can tell that the Holy Spirit leads him. This specific Sunday was different for our church. My pastor felt that our congregation needed encouragement from the Holy Spirit Himself. So instead of preaching, we spent the whole service worshiping and praying, and if a person wanted to be prayed for or wanted a touch from the Holy Spirit, they would go to the front and our pastor and some elders of the church would pray for them. To be honest, sometimes I am a little hesitant when we do this kind of service because I grew up knowing nothing about the gifts of the Spirit. I was and still am learning about how God moves.

There was quite a line of people who wanted a touch at this service. I was fine just worshiping and praying. However, I kept feeling I needed to go up to the front. And the feeling kept getting stronger and stronger. My heart was beating out of my chest; I was sweating but getting chills simultaneously. So I took a leap of faith and walked up to the front. Some individuals were still in line, so I just stood there and prayed. Keep in mind that our church service went from 10:30 to noon, and at this point it was 12:30. But I kept waiting. When it was my turn to get prayed for, I went up and my pastor asked what I wanted prayer for. I was thinking, *I thought you were just going to start praying!* LOL. I said I didn't know because I hadn't thought of anything. And I kid you not, the Holy Spirit told my pastor to say to me that He was pleased with the decision I had made. When I say that waterfalls were coming from my eyes, I am not kidding. All that pain and complicated decision-making. All that fighting God's plan until surrendering it all. All that mistrust turned into being fully committed to Him. It was worth it. To hear that the Lord of all was pleased with me changed everything.

I had some moments of weakness when my throwing coach would ask me to go to a meet and throw the javelin, and I would say yes because I felt desired and couldn't let go of the track goals I had set for myself. Then came summer! I worked at Midland all summer long. I did YMCA group fitness classes and was happy with my decision to step away. One day I went for ice cream with some friends who had also stayed over the summer, and they were talking about their practices and training, and I felt so left out. I immediately thought I had made the wrong decision. So right after that, I started training because, heck, I was going to start running again in the fall. Prayer after prayer, I asked God for clarity. I didn't quite know what He wanted me to do. If He wanted me to stop doing track, why would He want me to pick it up again?

A month later, I was walking and talking to a friend on the phone, and I asked her a question about praying. The phrase "write a book" came to my mind right after the question left my mouth. I couldn't stop thinking about it. So I prayed and prayed. I asked God to use me. I asked if He wanted me to write a book. I wondered what He wanted me to write about. Then the phrase "God-centered life" came to mind, and so did Philippians 4:8 (ESV), which says, "Whatever is true, whatever is honorable, whatever is just, whatever is pure, whatever is lovely, whatever is commendable, if there is any excellence, if there is anything worthy of praise, think about these things." So I prayed some more because I didn't want to do anything if God was not in it. I prayed for clarification or a sign that He wanted me to do this. Two days later, as I was unpacking my desk items for my dorm room, I found a bookmark from a Bible study I was a part of the year before. Attached to that bookmark, I found a sticky note. You will never guess what the sticky note had on it. It had the Philippians 4:8 verse written on it. And then after that, the verse kept popping up everywhere I went. *Okay, God, I hear you.* So with this book, I hope to show you that whatever is true, honorable, just, pure, lovely, commendable, excellent, and praiseworthy is God, and having Him at the center of your life makes life worth living.

Introduction

"Finally, brothers, whatever is true, whatever is honorable, whatever is just, whatever is pure, whatever is lovely, whatever is commendable, if there is any excellence, if there is anything worthy of praise, think about these things" (Philippians 4:8 ESV). These words from Philippians 4:8 have the power to transform minds and hearts, yet so often we read them and move on without letting them take root in our daily lives.

This book is an invitation to slow down and dwell in these powerful words of Paul—not just to read them but to live them. Each chapter explores one of these divine qualities: truth, honor, justice, purity, loveliness, commendableness, excellence, and praiseworthiness. But this isn't just another book to passively consume. It's meant to inspire a journey of transformation, carefully designed to help you not only understand these qualities but embody them.

The apostle Paul didn't just tell us to think about these things—he challenged us to practice them. That's why each chapter is paired with a journaling section, creating space for deep reflection and practical application. This is where the real transformation happens, where divine truth meets daily life.

In a world where our thoughts are constantly bombarded by negativity, fear, and doubt, these eight qualities serve as anchors for our minds. They're not just nice ideas—they're weapons against the enemy's attempts to derail us from our God-given purpose. As children of God, we have been given the authority to take every thought captive and align it with His truth.

So take your time with these pages. Let each word sink deep. Be honest in your reflections. Whether you're struggling with negative thought patterns, seeking spiritual growth, or simply wanting to align your mind more closely with God's truth, this journey is for you. Through these timeless qualities, may you discover the freedom that comes when we fix our thoughts on the things of God.

Your journey to freedom begins now. Let's walk this path together, one divine quality at a time.

1

True

THINK

ruth. It's a word that carries immense weight in our modern world, where competing voices clamor for our attention and different versions of reality clash daily on our social media feeds. As I sit down to write this chapter, I find myself wrestling with a familiar feeling of inadequacy. I'm just a normal girl living her life, and sometimes I wonder, *Who am I to write this book?* But then I remember what God says in Psalm 46:5—He is with me and won't let me fall. This reminder grounds me in what is true, not what my insecurities whisper to me in moments of doubt.

The concept of truth has been central to human existence since the beginning. In the garden of Eden, the very first deception occurred when Satan questioned God's truth: "Did God really say . . . ?" (Genesis 3:1). This question marked the beginning of humanity's struggle with truth versus lies, a battle that continues to rage in our hearts and minds today. Eve's fatal mistake wasn't just believing a lie; it was choosing to act independently of God's truth, a pattern that we often repeat in our own lives.

The Bible is filled with stories of people grappling with truth. Consider Thomas, who struggled to believe the truth of Jesus's resurrection until he could see and touch Jesus's wounds (John 20:24–29). His doubt wasn't just skepticism; it was a deep wrestle with truth that many of us can relate to. When Jesus appeared to Thomas, He didn't condemn him but instead offered the proof Thomas needed while gently encouraging a faith that believes without seeing.

Or think about Nathanael, who initially doubted anything good could come from Nazareth (John 1:46) but later proclaimed Jesus as the Son of God. His journey from skepticism to belief shows how encountering truth transforms our perspective entirely. Then there's Peter, who declared the truth about Jesus's identity as the Messiah (Matthew 16:16) yet later denied knowing Him three times (Luke 22:54–62). These stories remind us that even those closest to Jesus struggled with believing and living in truth.

Consider also the woman at the well, who encountered truth incarnate and couldn't help but share it with others (John 4:1–42). When Jesus spoke truth about her life, instead of running from it, she ran toward it and became one of the first evangelists in the New Testament. Her story teaches us that when we encounter real truth, it compels us to share that truth with others.

I've experienced this struggle firsthand during my college years. As a freshman, I found myself lost in a web of lies about who I was and what mattered. I went to frat parties, drank, and hung out with the wrong people, all while knowing deep down that I was straying from God's truth. I wanted to be accepted by my teammates so badly that I was willing to compromise what I knew to be true. The parties and the drinking made me feel like I belonged, but they left me feeling guilty and dirty inside. Through God's grace and the mentors He placed in my life, I found my way back to His truth.

The journey back wasn't easy. Each step required confronting another lie I'd believed about myself, about God, about what would make me happy. But as I began to align my life with God's truth again, I discovered something beautiful: truth doesn't just convict us; it liberates us. Jesus said, "You will know the truth, and the truth will set you free" (John 8:32 ESV). I experienced this firsthand as I eventually watched the chains of peer pressure and false identity fall away.

The enemy of our souls is strategic in how he attacks truth in our lives. He knows that if he can get us to question what's true about God, ourselves, and our purpose, he can lead us down paths of destruction. Think about how he operated in the garden of Eden. He didn't start with an outright lie, but with a question that made Eve doubt what she knew to be true. He uses the same tactics today with us, planting seeds of doubt about God's goodness, His plans for us, and our identity in Him.

I've seen this play out in my own battle with body image and self-worth. How many times have I looked in the mirror and believed the lie that I was too fat or too ugly? The truth is that I am fearfully and wonderfully made (Psalm 139:14), created in God's image for His purposes. Yet the enemy works overtime to make us forget this fundamental truth. He whispers lies that we're not enough, that we need to change ourselves to be worthy of love or acceptance.

In today's world, truth seems more relative than ever. Popular phrases like "my body, my choice" compete with biblical truth that declares our bodies are temples of the Holy Spirit (1 Corinthians 6:19). Social media feeds us constant messages about who we should be and what we should look like, making it increasingly difficult to focus on what God says is true. After being in school and looking back, I've seen how these competing messages can overwhelm and confuse even those of us raised in strong Christian homes.

The pressure to conform to the world's version of truth is immense. I have seen it in the classroom when biblical truth was challenged by secular philosophies. I feel it in social situations when standing for truth might mean standing alone. But here's what I've learned: truth isn't determined by majority vote. Truth isn't what feels right in the moment or what's currently popular. Truth is a Person—Jesus Christ.

But here's what's also true: God's Word stands unchanging amid the shifting sands of cultural truth. Jesus declared Himself to be "the way, and the truth, and the life" (John 14:6 ESV). This wasn't just a nice saying; it was a declaration that in Him we find absolute truth. When Jesus stood before Pilate, He said,

"For this purpose I was born and for this purpose I have come into the world—to bear witness to the truth. Everyone who is of the truth listens to my voice" (John 18:37 ESV).

The truth about Jesus is the foundation of all other truths. He came as God in flesh, born of a virgin, lived a perfect life, died for our sins, and rose again. This historical truth changes everything about how we view ourselves and our world. Because of Jesus's sacrifice, we no longer need the complex system of animal sacrifices that the Old Testament required. He became our perfect sacrifice, our lamb without blemish, making it possible for us to have a direct relationship with God.

Think about the significance of this truth. In the Old Testament, people had to constantly bring sacrifices to atone for their sins. There were specific sacrifices for specific sins, and the process never ended because people never stopped sinning. But Jesus's sacrifice was once and for all (Hebrews 10:10). This truth means we don't have to earn our way to God or constantly try to make up for our failures. We can rest in the finished work of Christ.

Our minds are battlegrounds where truth and lies compete daily. The Enemy wants us to take God out of the equation, but as I've learned through my own struggles, there would be no equation without God! "For from Him and through Him and to Him are all things" (Romans 11:36 ESV). When we find ourselves spiraling into anxiety or fear, it's often because we're engaging in what I call "wrongly focused meditation"—taking God out of the equation entirely.

I remember sitting at the lake during our team bonding event, unable to put on a swimsuit because I was so consumed by lies about my body. The tears that followed in my dorm room led to one of the most important conversations of my life with my mentor. She helped me see that criticizing myself was actually criticizing God's masterpiece. Imagine showing a child's drawing to them and calling it ugly—how crushing would that be to their spirit! Yet we do this to God's creation—ourselves—all the time.

This truth transformed how I saw myself. Instead of focusing on perceived flaws, I began to see myself as God's handiwork, created in Christ Jesus for good works that He prepared before I was born (Ephesians 2:10). This shift didn't happen overnight, and I still have moments of struggle, but now I have truth to combat the lies.

The truth is, we are human and we make mistakes. I've made plenty of them, but I know that God forgives and still loves. His love is everlasting (Jeremiah 31:3), and He has blotted out the sins of our past (Romans 8:1–2). This truth isn't just comforting; it's transformative when we really believe it. It means that no mistake is too big for God's grace, no sin beyond His forgiveness, no person beyond His love.

Think about the prodigal son (Luke 15:11–32). He believed lies about where he could find happiness and fulfillment. He wanted his inheritance early, essentially telling his father, "I wish you were dead." Yet when he returned home, his father ran to meet him, embraced him, and restored him to his position as son. This is the truth about God's love for us: it's not based on our performance but on His character.

Our true identity is not found in our accomplishments, our appearance, or our abilities. I learned this the hard way when I got caught up in my identity as a student-athlete. My entire introduction as an admissions ambassador for my school centered around being on the track team and studying education. When I retired from track (for a semester) and changed my major, I felt lost—until I remembered that my true identity is as a daughter of the King, and that will never change.

This identity crisis taught me something profound about truth: when we build our identity on anything other than God's truth, we're building on shifting sand. Accomplishments fade, appearances change, abilities diminish, but our identity in Christ is eternal. We are chosen (Ephesians 1:4), adopted (Galatians 4:5), beloved (1 John 3:1), and secure in Him (Romans 8:38–39).

The Holy Spirit plays a crucial role in helping us discern and live in truth. Jesus called Him the "Spirit of truth" and promised that He would guide us into all truth (John 14:17; 15:26; 16:13). This is why reading God's Word isn't just an academic exercise; it's a spiritual encounter where the Spirit reveals truth to us.

When we read Scripture, the Spirit illuminates God's truth and helps us apply it to our lives.

Consider how the Spirit worked in the early church. In Acts 2, when Peter preached at Pentecost, it was the Spirit of truth who convicted people's hearts and led them to accept the truth about Jesus. The same Spirit works in us today, helping us distinguish truth from lies and empowering us to live according to God's truth.

To live in truth, we need practical strategies. When thoughts enter our minds, we must

- identify the thought and determine if it aligns with God's truth,
- speak to that thought in Jesus's name,
- claim the truth of Scripture, and
- walk in that truth through our actions.

These aren't just nice suggestions; they're spiritual warfare tactics. Paul tells us in 2 Corinthians 10:5 (ESV) to "take every thought captive to obey Christ." This means actively comparing our thoughts against the truth of God's Word and rejecting anything that doesn't align with His truth.

True worship flows from accepting and living in God's truth. Jesus taught that "true worshipers will worship the Father in spirit and truth" (John 4:23 ESV). This kind of worship isn't just about singing songs or attending church; it's about aligning our entire lives with God's truth. When we live in truth, our whole life becomes an act of worship.

This truth-based worship affects every area of our lives. It influences how we treat others, how we handle our resources, how we make decisions. It means being honest in our relationships, ethical in our work, and faithful in our commitments. True worship is living out God's truth in the everyday moments of life.

Jesus described Himself as the "true vine" (John 15:1), emphasizing our need to stay connected to Him to bear fruit. Just as branches cannot survive when separated from their vine, we cannot thrive when disconnected from the source of all truth. He is also the "true light" (John 1:9), illuminating our path and exposing lies that would lead us astray.

Think about a vine and its branches. The branches don't strain or struggle to produce fruit; they simply stay connected to the vine, and fruit naturally follows. In the same way, when we stay connected to Jesus, the Truth, we naturally begin to reflect His truth in our lives. We don't have to strive or struggle to find truth; we just need to stay connected to Him who is Truth.

The truth also sets us free from the need to pretend or perform. When we know who we are in Christ, we don't have to put on a show for others or try to earn God's love. We can be authentic because we're secure in His truth. This freedom allows us to be honest about our struggles while maintaining hope in God's promises.

In our relationships with others, truth must be spoken in love (Ephesians 4:15). This means being honest but not harsh, truthful but not tactless. When we understand how God's truth has transformed our own lives, we can share it with others in a way that draws them to Him rather than pushing them away.

I want you to know that if you're struggling with lies from the Enemy, you're not alone. Whether it's lies about your worth, your past, your future, or your identity, God's truth is stronger. The Enemy hates truth because he knows it's what sets us free (John 8:32). But we have something he doesn't; we have the Truth Himself living inside us through His Spirit.

Remember, whatever is true comes from God's Word. Our thoughts have power, but we have power over our thoughts through Christ. When we focus on what is true— God's character, His promises, His love, and our identity in Him—everything else falls into proper perspective. In a world of relative truth, we can stand firm on the absolute truth of God's Word and His unchanging character.

The journey to living in truth is ongoing. There will be days when lies seem louder than truth, when doubts feel stronger than faith. But God's truth remains constant, and His Spirit continues to guide us into all truth. I encourage you to make Philippians 4:8 your daily filter: "Finally, brothers and sisters, whatever is true . . ." Let truth be the foundation upon which you build your life, and watch how God uses that foundation to transform every area of your existence.

Understanding truth in today's world requires us to look at how Jesus interacted with truth throughout His ministry. When He stood before Pilate, the Roman governor asked, "What is truth?" (John 18:38). This question echoes through the centuries to our present day. Pilate stood face-to-face with Truth incarnate yet couldn't recognize Him. How often do we do the same? We search for truth in self-help books, social media influencers, and popular philosophies while missing the Truth standing right before us.

Let's explore some of Jesus's profound statements about truth. When He said, "I am the way, and the truth, and the life" (John 14:6 ESV), He wasn't just making a theological statement; He was declaring that truth is fundamentally personal. Truth isn't just a concept or a set of facts; it's a Person we can know and relate to. This changes everything about how we approach truth in our daily lives.

I remember wrestling with this concept during my senior year of college. I was taking a philosophy class where we discussed different theories of truth: correspondence theory, coherence theory, pragmatic theory. My head was spinning with all these intellectual approaches to truth. Then one day, during my quiet time, I read John 14:6 again, and it hit me: while these philosophical discussions had their place, I knew Truth personally. I had experienced Him. This realization transformed how I approached my studies and my faith.

The Bible also shows us how truth intersects with everyday life through the story of Daniel and his friends. They faced immense pressure to compromise their beliefs in Babylon, but they chose to stand firm in God's truth. When offered the king's food, they didn't argue or rebel; they simply proposed a test based on truth (Daniel 1:11–16). Their story teaches us that standing for truth doesn't always mean confrontation; sometimes it means quietly living out what we know to be true and letting the results speak for themselves.

Speaking of results, let's talk about how truth affects our relationships. I've noticed in my own life that relationships built on anything less than truth eventually crumble. During my freshman year, I had friendships based on partying and superficial connections. They felt good at the moment but couldn't withstand the test of time or trials. In contrast, the friendships I've built around shared faith in God's truth have only grown stronger through challenges.

This reminds me of the friendship between David and Jonathan in the Bible. Their relationship was founded on truth—truth about God, truth about their circumstances, and truth in their communication with each other. Even when Jonathan's father, King Saul, was trying to kill David, Jonathan stood by the truth and protected his friend (1 Samuel 20). This kind of truth-based friendship is rare but invaluable.

The connection between truth and love is another crucial aspect we need to explore. Sometimes people pit truth against love, as if we have to choose between being truthful and being loving. But Scripture shows us that true love and truth are inseparable. First Corinthians 13:6 tells us that love "rejoices with the truth." When we truly love someone, we want what's true for them, not just what makes them feel good momentarily.

I learned this lesson through a difficult situation with my good friend. She was making choices that I knew were harmful to her, and I had to decide: would I stay quiet to keep the peace, or would I speak the truth in love? After much prayer, I chose to have an honest conversation with her. It was uncomfortable at first, but that conversation became a turning point in both our relationship and her life. True love doesn't avoid truth; it embraces it.

Truth also plays a vital role in our mental and emotional health. In my own struggle with anxiety and body image issues, I discovered that the root of many mental health challenges lies in believing lies rather than truth. When we believe lies about ourselves, others, or God, it affects our entire well-being. This is why renewing our minds with God's truth is so crucial (Romans 12:2).

The Psalms give us a beautiful picture of how to process our emotions through the lens of truth. David often starts each of his psalms by pouring out his raw emotions—fear, anger, depression—but he always brought those feelings back to the truth of who God is. In Psalm 42:5 (ESV), he asks himself, "Why are you cast down, O my soul?" Then, in the same verse, he reminds himself, "Hope in God; for I shall again praise him, my salvation and my God." The truth here is that we can hope in God and He gives us salvation.

This pattern of emotional honesty combined with truth-based thinking has been revolutionary in my own life. When I feel overwhelmed by negative thoughts about my body or my worth, I've learned to do what David did—acknowledge the feelings but then actively remind myself of God's truth. It's not about denying our emotions; it's about anchoring them in truth.

Let's talk about truth in the context of spiritual warfare, because that's exactly what it is. Paul tells us in Ephesians 6:14 to put on the "belt of truth" as part of our spiritual armor. Why a belt? In Roman military gear, the belt held everything else together. Similarly, truth is what holds all other aspects of our spiritual life together. Without truth, our faith becomes unstable, our peace uncertain, and our righteousness compromised.

I've experienced this spiritual warfare firsthand, especially in moments of decision-making. When I was considering changing my major, the enemy attacked with lies: *You're letting everyone down. You're wasting your potential. You'll never succeed in a different field.* But God's truth cut through these lies like a sword: "I know the plans I have for you" (Jeremiah 29:11). "I will instruct you and teach you in the way you should go" (Psalm 32:8).

The truth about spiritual warfare is that it's not always dramatic. Sometimes it's as subtle as a slight distortion of God's Word—just like Satan's approach in the garden of Eden. This is why we need to be thoroughly grounded in scriptural truth. When I started memorizing Scripture seriously, I noticed I became much more sensitive to subtle deviations from truth in the messages I heard around me.

Truth also has a purifying effect on our lives. Jesus prayed, "Sanctify them in the truth; your word is truth" (John 17:17 ESV). This means that as we align ourselves with God's truth, we naturally become more like Him. It's not about trying harder to be good; it's about letting truth transform us from the inside out.

I saw this transformation in action through my mentor's life. She had gone through similar struggles as I had with identity and worth in her college years, but years of walking in God's truth had changed her. Her life wasn't perfect, but there was an authenticity and peace about her that I wanted. She showed me that embracing truth is a journey, not a destination.

The relationship between truth and freedom is another crucial aspect we need to understand. Jesus said, "You will know the truth, and the truth will set you free" (John 8:32). But what kind of freedom was He talking about? Not just freedom from obvious sins, but freedom from false beliefs, toxic thought patterns, and the pressure to perform for others' approval.

I experienced this freedom when I finally embraced the truth about God's grace. For years, I tried to earn God's love through perfect behavior and religious activities. I was essentially living in bondage to performance. When the truth of grace finally sank in—that God loved me because of who He is, not because of what I do—it was like chains falling off. I could finally serve God from a place of love rather than fear.

This brings us to an important point about discernment. In a world full of competing voices and claims to truth, how do we know what's really true? The Bible gives us several keys:

- Does it align with Scripture? (2 Timothy 3:16–17)
- Does it point to Jesus? (John 16:13–14)
- Does it produce good fruit in our lives? (Matthew 7:15–20)
- Has it been confirmed by wise counsel? (Proverbs 11:14)

I've learned to apply these tests to everything I hear, whether it's a sermon, a social media post, or advice from a friend. Truth that comes from God will always align with His character and His Word.

Let's also address the relationship between truth and community. While truth is absolute and not determined by consensus, God has designed us to discover and live out truth in community with other believers. The early church devoted themselves to the apostles' teaching (truth) and to fellowship (Acts 2:42). These two elements—truth and community—worked together to establish and grow the church.

I've experienced this in my own life through my church's Bible study group. When we study Scripture together, everyone brings different insights and perspectives, helping us all see truth more clearly. There's something powerful about discovering truth in a community that goes beyond what we can learn on our own.

The role of the Holy Spirit in guiding us into truth cannot be overstated. Jesus called Him the Spirit of truth and promised that He would guide us into all truth (John 16:13). This guidance isn't just about understanding theological concepts—it's about applying truth to our specific situations and challenges.

I remember a time when I was struggling with forgiveness toward someone who had hurt me deeply. I knew the truth that I should forgive, but I felt unable to do it. As I prayed, the Holy Spirit brought to mind the truth of how much God had forgiven me, and suddenly forgiveness wasn't just a concept; it became possible through His power, and it's something He calls us to do.

Truth also plays a crucial role in worship. Jesus said that true worshippers must worship in spirit and truth (John 4:23). This means our worship must be based on true knowledge of God, not just emotional experiences or cultural traditions. When we worship God for who He truly is—not just who we imagine Him to be—our worship becomes deeper and more meaningful.

This has changed how I approach worship, whether in church or in my personal devotions. Instead of just singing songs based on how they make me feel, I've learned to focus on the truth they proclaim about God's character and actions. This truth-based worship has transformed my relationship with God.

The truth about our identity in Christ is particularly relevant in today's world of personal branding and carefully curated social media personas. The world tells us to create our own identity, but God's truth tells us we already have one—we are His beloved children (1 John 3:1), chosen and adopted into His family (Ephesians 1:4–5).

This truth has practical implications for how we live. When we know who we truly are in Christ, we don't need to pretend to be someone else. We don't need to chase after approval or validation from others. We can live authentically because our identity is secure in Him.

As we conclude this exploration of truth, let me share one final personal story. Last year, I was asked to speak at a campus event about my faith journey. As I prepared, I felt those familiar feelings of inadequacy creeping in. But then I remembered where we started—with the truth that God is with me and won't let me fall (Psalm 46:5). This truth gave me the courage to share openly about my struggles and victories, and God used my story to impact others.

That's the power of truth—it not only transforms our own lives but also enables us to help others find freedom. In a world of relative truth and shifting standards, we have the privilege of knowing and sharing absolute truth found in God's Word and ultimately in Jesus Christ Himself.

Remember, the journey of living in truth is ongoing. There will be days when lies seem louder than truth, when doubts feel stronger than faith. But God's truth remains constant, and His Spirit continues to guide us. As we choose to believe and live according to what is true, we'll experience the freedom, peace, and purpose that come from aligning our lives with God's truth.

So I challenge you: What lies are you believing today? What truths from God's Word do you need to embrace? Take some time to write them down, pray over them, and ask the Holy Spirit to help you walk in truth. Remember, you're not alone in this journey. God is with you, and His truth will always prevail.

PRACTICE

Philippians 4:8 instructs us to think about all these traits, but the writer of the book follows that verse with a challenge. He tells believers that they need to practice these things as well. Honestly, I have battled the need to practice them. I would literally procrastinate practicing them by doing other tasks instead, like cleaning, going for a workout, hanging out with friends, or making a phone call. After a bunch of self-reflection, I realized that I was afraid. I was afraid that God wouldn't respond or hear me. I was also afraid of missing out on things with my friends. But most of all, I was afraid that my heavenly Father would reject me. Father wounds are hard for most of us to overcome, and inevitably, my experiences with my earthly father had spilled over to my heavenly Father. Although my relationship with my father is healing, there was quite a bit I had to work through, with him and on my own. I was putting God in a box. You guys, healing is a process, and it takes time and a lot of prayers. But by practicing what was true and changing my thoughts to revolve around God and His Word, I began to accelerate the process.

Let me explain how to practice what is true. Pulling what I said earlier in the chapter about our thoughts and identity, I will break it down. I already gave you some steps to win the battle of your mind, but there is more.

Our minds, thoughts, and attitude have a huge influence on our lives. Whatever is occupying our mind will eventually work its way out into our words and actions. This can be very destructive to you and the people around you if your thoughts are not truth based. The only way to capture your thoughts is to recognize when a thought is not God honoring and then replace the thought with the counter truth from God's Word. All of His Word is truth. Worldly things are not the truth and will only make you spiral into a deeper hole. In this section, I have given you some space below to write down the untrue thoughts that you struggle with the most. This can be anything from thoughts you have about yourself to bad thoughts about others to thoughts that destroy your view of God.

Take a look at the thoughts you've written. You don't have to share them with anyone, but you might want to pray about them. God knows your deepest thoughts and He cares, but He loves when you give those thoughts to Him. Now turn to the Bible. Look up verses that flip those untrue thoughts into something true that God says. Write them down and look at them so often that when a thought comes into your mind that is not true, it will automatically go to God's Word, which is truth.

JOURNAL

_____

_____

_____

_____

_____

_____

_____

_____

_____

_____

_____

_____

_____

_____

_____

_____

_____

_____

_____

_____

_____

_____

_____

2

Honorable

THINK

*I*n our modern world, the concept of honor often feels antiquated, relegated to period dramas and historical tales of knights and nobles. Yet true honor—the kind that stems from genuine devotion to what is right and good—remains as relevant today as it ever was. The Bible speaks extensively about honor, particularly in relation to our relationship with God. At its core, what is truly honorable is deserving of both respect and worship. And as we delve deeper into this truth, we discover that genuine worship belongs to God alone.

Throughout Scripture, we encounter a profound theme: our God is a jealous God. This divine jealousy isn't the petty, insecure kind we might associate with human relationships. Rather, it's the righteous desire of a loving Creator who knows that letting anything else take His rightful place in our lives will ultimately lead to our detriment. In Exodus 34:14, God declares, "Do not worship any other god, for the LORD, whose name is Jealous, is a jealous God." This characteristic of God isn't a flaw or weakness; it's an expression of His perfect love and desire for our highest good.

When we elevate anything above God—be it career ambitions, relationships, material success, or even noble pursuits—we engage in a subtle form of idol worship. I learned this lesson the hard way when I wanted to look perfect. I was so determined to prove myself that I regularly skipped reading my Bible to go to the gym, justified missing small group to rest for my health, and gradually replaced my prayer time with creating perfect meal plans. It wasn't until a mentor pointed out how my priorities had shifted that I realized I had made my body an idol.

The challenge lies in how easily these substitutes can slip into God's position in our lives. We might find ourselves prioritizing professional excellence, pursuing academic achievements, chasing athletic goals, or becoming consumed by social media's endless scroll. Last summer I noticed how my Instagram habit had slowly taken over my morning devotional time. What started as "just five minutes" of scrolling turned into an hour of mindlessly comparing my life to carefully curated highlights of others. The Holy Spirit convicted me that I was seeking validation from likes and comments rather than finding my worth in God's unchanging love.

I've also experienced this struggle intensely during my college years. My desire for academic excellence, while admirable in itself, began to overshadow my spiritual life. The pursuit of straight A's and a spot on the school president's list became all-consuming. I found myself prioritizing month-ahead projects over time in God's Word, justifying my choices with the seemingly noble goal of academic achievement. It was a subtle shift but one that gradually eroded my spiritual foundation.

Looking back, I realize how easily we can rationalize our misplaced priorities. During my junior year, I remember sitting in the library at eleven o'clock at night, working on a research paper that wasn't due for weeks, while my Bible sat unopened in my dorm room. I kept telling myself I was just being responsible and diligent, but in reality I was slowly drifting from my first love, much like the church at Ephesus that Jesus addressed in Revelation 2:4.

This common struggle was perfectly captured in a poignant cartoon I once saw on a Christian social media page. The illustration depicted Jesus sitting at a restaurant table at different times of the day, waiting for someone named John. The scene begins at 8:00 a.m., with Jesus arriving early, anticipating John's arrival for coffee. I remember how the image struck me deeply because it reminded me of my own tendency to keep God waiting while I attended to "more urgent" matters.

As the day progresses in the cartoon—8:05 a.m., 8:45 a.m., 12:45 p.m.—Jesus continues to wait patiently, making gentle excuses for His friend's absence. Each time the waiter comes by, Jesus's response reveals His unfailing love and patience. It reminded me of the many times I've hit the snooze button on my alarm, promising to pray "later," only to find myself crawling into bed at night having never made time for God.

Finally, at 8:20 p.m., John hurriedly appears. Before Jesus can fully express His joy at seeing him, John launches into a rapid-fire monologue: "Jesus! Hey! Yeah, work is super stressful. Speaking of, can you help out with this project? And I'm still stuck between buying a house or staying in my apartment. Oh, and there's this girl at church—you know who—if it's your will, make things go smoothly. And heal the poor, help the sick, and all that. Gotta run—early start tomorrow!"[1]

I saw myself so clearly in John's behavior. Just last month I caught myself treating my prayer time like a drive-through window: rushing through my requests and barely pausing to listen for God's response. I was convicted about how often I approach God with my agenda rather than seeking His presence. The cartoon served as a powerful reminder that true relationships, whether human or divine, require intentional investment of time and attention from both parties.

The materialistic nature of our world compounds this challenge. We naturally gravitate toward what we can see, touch, and immediately experience. I notice this especially in my own prayer life. It's so much easier to focus on a friend sitting across from me at coffee than to quiet my mind and heart before an invisible God. But as I've learned to cultivate spiritual

---

[1] @jesus_the_lord_, "8:00 am," Instagram post, April 1, 2021, https://www.instagram.com/p/CNJEOpGD4rk/.

disciplines, I've discovered that God's invisible presence can become more real than physical reality.

Last week I experienced this truth powerfully during my morning prayer walk. Instead of listening to my usual podcast, I decided to simply walk in silence, focusing on God's presence. As I observed the sunrise, felt the breeze, and listened to the birds, I was overwhelmed by the reality that the Creator of all this beauty was walking with me. It was a vivid reminder that while God operates beyond our physical senses, His presence is more real and lasting than anything we can touch or see.

The concept of honor in Scripture is sometimes translated as "noble," which has always fascinated me. Growing up watching Disney princess movies, I was captivated by tales of nobility and royalty. I would spend hours in my backyard, wearing my fancy dresses and my plastic tiara, pretending to be a princess. My friends and I would create elaborate stories about royal balls and brave princes. Little did I understand then that through Christ I had already been granted a far greater royal status: adoption into God's family as a daughter of the King of Kings.

This truth became particularly meaningful to me during a difficult period in college when I was struggling with self-worth. My best friend had just gotten engaged, another friend had landed her dream job, and I was feeling increasingly uncertain about my future. One morning during my devotions, I read 1 Peter 2:9, which describes believers as "a royal priesthood, a holy nation, God's special possession." The Holy Spirit used that verse to remind me that my identity wasn't found in my relationship status or career prospects but in my position as a daughter of the King.

Speaking of identity, I've noticed how the world's definition of honor often differs markedly from God's perspective. Recently, I was having coffee with my friend Sarah, and we got into a discussion about what it means to be honorable. At first, she defined honor in terms of worldly achievement—getting into the Fortune 500, winning Olympic medals, earning prestigious degrees. But when I asked her what she thought honor meant from a biblical perspective, her whole demeanor changed.

"You know," she said, thoughtfully stirring her latte, "Jesus never seemed impressed by the things we typically celebrate. He spent time with lepers and tax collectors. He washed His disciples' feet. He honored people the world ignored." Her observation led us into a deep conversation about how Jesus's example challenges our modern metrics of success and honor.

This divine perspective on honor was beautifully illustrated during a recent sermon series at my church focusing on the Holy Spirit. Our guest speaker brought a mug of hot water and a tea bag to the pulpit one Sunday morning. As he spoke, he used these simple items to demonstrate a profound truth about the Holy Spirit's work in our lives.

The speaker explained that we are like the water, and the Holy Spirit is like the tea bag. Once the tea bag is introduced, the water is permanently changed—it can never revert to its original state. Similarly, when the Holy Spirit enters our lives, we are fundamentally transformed. I remember watching the clear water gradually take on the rich color of the tea, thinking about how my own life had been transformed since accepting Christ in high school.

But the illustration didn't stop there. The speaker pointed out that the longer the tea bag stays in the water, the stronger the tea becomes. Just as concentrated tea has a more robust flavor, our lives demonstrate more of God's character as we continue walking with Him. This truth was demonstrated in my own life when I went through a particularly challenging season at track practice last year, though the example might seem silly.

We were all contenders to run the 4-by-400-meter race, and the atmosphere was tense with uncertainty and fear. In the past, I would have been consumed by anxiety, but I found myself experiencing an unexpected peace. Years of walking with God and steeping in His presence had transformed my natural reactions. My teammates noticed the difference, which led to several meaningful conversations about faith.

Scripture provides numerous examples of honorable individuals whose lives demonstrate these principles. I've always been particularly moved by Joseph's story. During a period when I was facing workplace harassment, Joseph's example of maintaining his integrity despite Potiphar's wife's advances gave me courage to stand firm in my own ethical convictions.

The story of Ruth has also deeply impacted my life, especially during times when following God meant leaving comfortable situations. When I felt called to turn down a job opportunity to pursue ministry work, Ruth's words to Naomi echoed in my heart: "Where you go I will go, and where you stay I will stay. Your people will be my people and your God my God" (Ruth 1:16). Her example helped me trust God's leading, even when the path seemed uncertain.

King David's story has been particularly meaningful in teaching me about handling difficult relationships. During a period when I was dealing with an unfair boss, David's response to Saul's persecution provided a powerful model. Despite having opportunities for revenge, David chose to honor God's timing and authority. His example helped me maintain a respectful attitude even while seeking appropriate ways to address workplace issues.

Daniel's unwavering faithfulness in exile has inspired me during times when standing for my faith felt costly. Last year, when my team scheduled team-bonding activities during my church service time, Daniel's example of continuing to pray despite the king's decree gave me courage to respectfully request accommodation for my religious commitments.

But of course, Jesus Christ remains our ultimate example of honor. His life demonstrates that true honor often looks different from worldly success or recognition. It might mean choosing integrity over advantage, service over status, or sacrifice over comfort. I've found this particularly challenging in my social media use, where the temptation to present a perfectly curated image often conflicts with authentic Christian witness.

Recently, I made the decision to be more honest about my struggles and failures on my platforms, sharing not just the highlights but also the moments when I'm learning and growing. While this approach has meant fewer likes and followers, it's allowed for more meaningful connections and opportunities to point others to Christ.

The calling to live honorably remains as challenging and vital today as ever. In a world that often celebrates self-promotion and immediate gratification, choosing to honor God through faithful obedience may seem countercultural. However, like the tea bag transforming water, the Holy Spirit works within us, gradually conforming us to Christ's image and enabling us to live lives of true honor.

I don't know if you have ever had this happen, but recently I faced a small but significant choice between honesty and convenience. A cashier gave me too much change, and while the amount was minimal, the Holy Spirit prompted me to return it. As I explained the error to the surprised cashier, I was reminded that honor is built through these small, daily choices to align our actions with God's character.

This transformation isn't instantaneous or always easy, but it is guaranteed for those who continue seeking God. Each day presents new opportunities to choose honor – in our relationships, work, studies, and private moments. As we consistently choose God's way over worldly wisdom, we find ourselves becoming more like Jesus, the most honorable person who ever lived.

Let us therefore fix our eyes on Jesus, the author and perfecter of our faith, who modeled perfect honor in every aspect of His life. May we, like Him, choose to honor God above all else, knowing that true honor flows from a heart fully surrendered to His lordship. In doing so, we fulfill our highest calling as children of the King, reflecting His character to a world desperate for authentic demonstrations of honor.

This journey of living honorably is one we'll never fully complete on this side of heaven, but it's one worth pursuing with all our heart, soul, mind, and strength. As I have been writing this book, my prayer has been that readers will be inspired to seek true honor—not the fleeting recognition of the world but the lasting impact of a life lived in devotion to our King.

PRACTICE

Worship can be accomplished in many different ways, such as through prayer, singing praise, serving others, sharing your testimony, meditating on Scripture, giving, and journaling. In this section of practice, I will write a prayer that you can pray, and then I'll give you space to write your own prayer to praise God for how honorable and worthy He is.

Honorable God,

We praise You. You are the only God we want to worship and sing praises to all the days of our life. Thank You for creating in me a clean spirit oh God. Thank You for giving me the gift of the Holy Spirit. I want to carry that treasure with confidence all day every day. Thank You for leading me through this life and never leaving me. With all the sin and brokenness in the world, I'm praising You because You are my Savior. You are the only one who can heal the sick and fix all that is broken. What a praiseworthy God You are! Nothing is greater than You. Your love is greater than any other love. Your strength is able to help me through any situation. I worship You for allowing me to rest in Your presence and sit at Your feet. Jesus, thank You for taking my sin and all the sin of the world for the rest of eternity and dying an awful death, so we can have a relationship with God the Father. You are so honorable! Holy Spirit, thank You for filling me up and guiding me every step of the way. You give me power to do things my fleshly self would not do. God the Father, thank You for being perfect in all Your ways, in correcting, in loving, and in relationships. God, You are all I want to think about.

In your honorable name, Jesus. Amen.

Honorable

JOURNAL

3

Just

THINK

The morning rush at the coffee shop was in full swing when an angry customer stormed up to the counter, demanding to speak to a manager. Her drink wasn't made exactly as she wanted, and she wasn't shy about letting everyone know. As I watched the scene unfold, my immediate reaction was to judge her harshly, to write her off as just another difficult customer making a barista's life miserable. But in that moment, God's gentle conviction stopped me. Who was I to judge her story? Perhaps she was facing a crisis I knew nothing about. Perhaps she'd just received devastating news or lost her job. This simple moment in a coffee shop became a profound lesson about justice and judgment—one that would lead me to deeply examine what it means to think and act justly in a world quick to condemn.

That experience sparked a journey into understanding true biblical justice. I began to realize that justice isn't just about courtrooms and legal proceedings; it's about how we think about and treat others in our everyday moments. It's about seeing people the way God sees them and responding with both truth and grace.

The word *just* is defined by the *Oxford Dictionary* as "behaving according to what is morally right and fair," but as Christians, we must search the Scriptures and not a dictionary to define our requirement to act justly. In Micah 6:8, the Hebrew word for *just* is *mishpat*. This powerful word encompasses far more than our modern understanding of justice—it's an act of deciding a case, a place, court, seat of judgment, process, procedure, litigation before judges, and case or cause presented for judgment. Mishpat means so much more than just judging; it also means governing with righteousness and wisdom. The word *mishpat* is a two-edged sword. When we think of God as the judge, He is loving and wants the best for all His children, but He will judge everyone fairly according to what we do on Earth. Psalm 62:11–12 (ESV) says, "Once God has spoken; twice have I heard this; that power belongs to God, and that to you, O Lord, belongs steadfast love. For you will render to a man according to his work." God is all-powerful and all-knowing. He knows what you and I do behind closed doors. Nothing is hidden. When it comes our time to stand before God so He can judge us, what will He say to you? Are you walking the walk and talking the talk? God has the power to know our thoughts as well. Are you taking captive all your thoughts and directing them toward God and the truth?

When I first began studying the concept of mishpat, I was struck by a situation at my workplace that perfectly illustrated its depth. A senior manager was making decisions that benefited certain team members while disadvantaging others, particularly those from minority backgrounds. The injustice was subtle—masked behind corporate policies and procedures—but its impact was profound. As I wrestled with how to address this situation, I discovered that mishpat calls us not just to recognize injustice but to actively work toward making things right.

Moses, in the Bible, was called to be a judge. That position means he would proclaim ordinance, pass judgment, and carry it out to punishment or release. Like Moses, we, too, are called to understand and apply God's justice in our spheres of influence. This became clear to me during my time mentoring at-risk youth. One young person, Marcus, had been labeled a "troublemaker" by his teachers and peers. But as I got to know him, I discovered a brilliant mind struggling against systemic barriers and personal trauma. Mishpat required more than just acknowledging these injustices; it demanded action. Through advocacy, support, and genuine relationship-building, we helped Marcus access educational opportunities that had previously been denied to him.

It is at the seat of the divine throne that rights are given. God is on the throne. Do you have Him on the throne of your life? He is the only one worthy of being a judge. Any human being cannot judge. We have all made mistakes and fallen short of the glory of God. Our job is to love and point people toward Jesus, not judge or condemn, which would give people the wrong impression of what Jesus is like. It is hard, however, because as humans we are constantly judging others. We judge based on behaviors or how someone looks. We want to judge their character and whether or not they would be a good friend.

But what if we flipped the script and instead of judging a person from the moment we saw them, we thought of them as God's creation, created in His image? How would that change our thought process and the way we look at every single person we come in contact with? Let's let God be God and do His job and just rest in His presence, knowing that He has it all under control.

During my time as a student teacher, I encountered a situation that deeply challenged my understanding of justice. Two students were caught cheating—one from a privileged background with supportive parents, the other living in foster care and struggling with trauma. The school's zero-tolerance policy called for the same punishment for both, but was that truly just? This experience taught me that godly justice must consider context while maintaining standards, much like how God deals with each of us individually while upholding His perfect standards.

Another personal story comes to mind from my time volunteering at a local food bank. One afternoon a woman came in wearing designer clothes and driving an expensive car. My initial reaction, I'm ashamed to say, was judgment, wondering why someone who appeared wealthy would need food assistance. But God quickly convicted me of my unjust thinking. I later learned she had recently lost her husband, was struggling with medical bills, and was trying to keep her children in their school while searching for work. This experience taught me how easily we can make unfair assumptions about others without knowing their full story.

Another time, I witnessed injustice in my workplace when a coworker was being blamed for something they hadn't done. It would have been easier to stay quiet and avoid getting involved, but I knew that justice sometimes requires us to speak up, even when it's uncomfortable. With prayer and careful consideration, I approached our supervisor and shared what I knew about the situation. It wasn't easy, but it was right. The situation was resolved, and my coworker was cleared. This experience showed me that thinking justly often leads to acting justly, even when it costs us something.

The Bible tells us that God is just. This means that He is fair and impartial. It also means that He hates the mistreatment of people and of nature, all of which He has created. He hates lying, cheating, and other forms of oppression of others. The fact that God is just means that He can and will judge between right and wrong, and He will administer justice in accordance with His standards.

Many times in the Bible, God is pictured as a judge. The Bible says that He will one day judge the world. Many of us shy away from the thought of God as a judge because the examples of justice we see on Earth are flawed: some judges are corrupt, and even when their intentions are good, they can make mistakes. However, the fact that God is just assures us that when He acts as a judge, He will administer justice perfectly. His ability to do this involves other aspects, or attributes, of His character, including His ability to discern the truth in every situation and see into the hearts and minds of men. His wisdom, His strength, His authority, and His moral character—these all contribute to his ability to establish what is right and wrong.

A God who did not care about the difference between right and wrong and did not judge humans for acting one way or the other would not be an admirable being worthy of our love or trust. The fact that God is just and will judge between right and wrong gives ultimate moral significance to our lives and makes us accountable for our actions.

If there is an all-powerful, all-knowing Supreme Being who is inherently just and who will act as our judge, what does this mean for humans like you and me? It means that our actions on Earth and our attitudes toward God will ultimately be judged. This is a very serious concern since we have all fallen short of God's perfect standards and we must pay the penalty for those shortcomings (Romans 3:23; 6:23). Fortunately, we also know that God is a God of mercy.

In His mercy, He has provided a way for us to be reconciled with Him and to meet His standards. He has provided a substitute who was willing to pay our penalty if we are willing to accept that arrangement. He did this through the death of His Son, Jesus Christ, who died to cover the penalty we would have to pay for our wrongdoing (Romans 3:24). All we have to do is accept this substitution. Then the God who is both just and merciful will forgive and forget our shortcomings. The Bible tells us He will even accept us and treat us as His children and His heirs. When God presented His Son, Jesus, as a substitute to pay the penalty for our wrongdoing, the Bible says He did it to demonstrate His justice, "so as to be just and the one who justifies those who have faith in Jesus" (Romans 3:26).

Now you might be asking, if God is just, why do we see so much unfairness on Earth?

Where we see injustice on Earth, it is at the hands of men, not of God. God has given men free will, but most men do not exercise it responsibly or in a way that lines up with God's character as a just God. As discussed above, the time will come when God will judge the world and the people in it. He will dispose of evil and injustice, and He will punish those who have turned away from Him and His standards. However, in His wisdom, He is not doing that yet. The apostle Peter tells us that God is waiting because He is patient and wants everyone to have an opportunity to accept His Son's sacrifice rather than paying the penalty that justice requires for their sins (2 Peter 3:9).

Some other examples of where God is just in the Bible is in the book of Habakkuk. Habakkuk complains to God that his people are ignoring his demand for justice, and he wonders why God allows the unjust to continue in their wickedness: "Why do you make me look at injustice? Why do you tolerate wrongdoing? Destruction and violence are before me; there is strife, and conflict abounds. Therefore the law is paralyzed, and justice never prevails" (Habakkuk 1:3–4). Habakkuk asks how God's justice can reconcile with his experience of the world. God's answer is that He has appointed "the Babylonians, that ruthless and impetuous people," to punish his rebellious children by taking them into exile (Habakkuk 1:6).

Another example is with Adam and Eve, who were told by God, "But you must not eat from the tree of the knowledge of good and evil, for when you eat from it you will certainly die" (Genesis 2:17). Adam and Eve became sinful and no longer eternal beings on Earth because of sin. God judged them for their sin, but still loved them enough to bring more people into the earth.

Matthew 18:21–35 is the parable of the unforgiving servant. In this passage, Peter is asking God how many times he should forgive someone who sins against him. Jesus uses this opportunity to teach that though God's forgiveness is given freely to those who confess and turn from their sins, we must also be willing to forgive others. Even though others do harm to us, we are called to forgive and love. God will do to them as they deserve, but He will also do to us as we deserve if we don't forgive them.

Luke 16:19–31 contains the parable about the rich man and Lazarus. The rich man lived his whole life being self-centered and making wrong choices. When the rich man died, he went to Hades, which is where the wicked go until the final judgment. Lazarus was a poor man who lived in poverty, but his heart was right with God. He never gave up faith. When Lazarus died, he went to heaven until the final judgment. This parable shows that in the end, God will make all things right. Those who live for themselves on Earth will end in a place of eternal torment. Those who live for God will end up in paradise and be in His presence forever. Even though on Earth it seems that rich people have everything, in the end they will have nothing. God gives His treasures to His faithful followers. He doesn't care about outward appearances, fame, or gifts; He cares about the heart posture. He is just and will give everyone as each deserves. Once we die, our eternal destination is final.

Matthew 7:1–2 says "Judge not, that you be not judged. For with the judgment you pronounce you will be judged, and with the measure you use it will be measured to you." Jesus condemns our habit of criticizing others while ignoring our own faults. Judging in an unjust manner also includes rejecting or condemning someone who is doing wrong without genuinely desiring to see that person turn to God and accept forgiveness. Having that attitude is the same as wishing God's judgment on someone without having them first receive God's mercy.

This passage is not saying that we should not correct sin, though. If someone is sinning in the church, it is biblical to correct them in love. If someone in the world is sinning, we shouldn't attack them because it will only lead to greater resistance. For them, we should lead by example instead. Calling out sin and judging others for their sins are two different things. Calling out people for their sins is a way of showing someone you love them because you want them to correct their ways so they can have a closer relationship with God. Sin is what separates us from God, so why would we not help a brother or sister recognize when they are living in sin? Judging someone for their sins is not what we are called to do, and God says that we will be judged the same way with the same measures.

Isaiah 33:22 says, "The LORD is our judge; the LORD is our lawgiver; the LORD is our king; he will save us." We do not submit to any ungodly order; the Lord is whom we submit to. He is whom we ultimately surrender our life to for judgment. We should not put anyone else on the "throne" of our life. This is why we must pray for the people in leadership in our country. We need to pray that the Holy Spirit leads them. If any law is passed that is unbiblical, we must follow God's law, not the world's.

Second Thessalonians 1:6–7 says, "God is just: He will pay back trouble to those who trouble you and give relief to you who are troubled, and to us as well.

This will happen when the Lord Jesus is revealed from heaven in blazing fire with his powerful angels." We are called to show others love and to forgive those who wrong us. This can be very hard, but there is peace in knowing that God will serve justice whether the wrongdoer receives a natural consequence in this life or God addresses the wrongdoing with them when they die. Nothing goes unnoticed by God.

Matthew 7–15 (ESV) says,

"Judge not, that you be not judged. For with the judgment you pronounce you will be judged, and with the measure you use it will be measured to you. Why do you see the speck that is in your brother's eye, but do not notice the log that is in your own eye? Or how can you say to your brother, 'Let me take the speck out of your eye,' when there is the log in your own eye? You hypocrite, first take the log out of your own eye, and then you will see clearly to take the speck out of your brother's eye."

We are also sinners and cannot judge another man's heart like God can. Does this mean we shouldn't keep each other accountable in addressing sin with each other? Absolutely not. It means we should not do this with a critical spirit and should prioritize addressing our own sin first. We are forgiven sinners, and we should approach others in a manner of grace and truth. It is not our job to be the judge of their lives.

Micah 6:8 says, "He has shown you, O mortal, what is good. And what does the LORD require of you? To act justly and to love mercy and to walk humbly with your God." Be impartial. As disciples of Jesus, acting justly means making fair decisions in both our professional and personal lives. James instructs us not to show favoritism to beautiful, "important," or rich people (James 2:1–13). Also, Leviticus 19:15 says, "Do not pervert justice; do not show partiality to the poor or favoritism to the great, but judge your neighbor fairly."

Be accurate in your judgments of yourself as well. Truthful living means I refuse to exaggerate to make myself look better than my actions prove I really am. I deceive only myself when I try to rationalize my decisions or behavior.

We should be focused on living lives like Jesus did. In Matthew 16:27, Jesus said, "For the Son of Man is going to come in his Father's glory with his angels, and then he will reward each person according to what they have done." We need to live with eternity in mind as believers! Let's make heaven crowded and be the hands and feet of Jesus on this earth!

Scripture provides a vivid portrayal of this final judgement. Revelation 20:12–15 (ESV) says,

> And I saw the dead, great and small, standing before the throne, and books were opened. Then another book was opened, which is the book of life. And the dead were judged by what was written in the books, according to what

they had done. And the sea gave up the dead who were in it, Death and Hades gave up the dead who were in them, and they were judged, each one of them, according to what they had done. Then Death and Hades were thrown into the lake of fire. This is the second death, the lake of fire. And if anyone's name was not found written in the book of life, he was thrown into the lake of fire.

We must remember that God is always just. It is part of His character. He's fair and will pay back the righteous, and fools will get what they deserve in the end. This divine justice, while sobering for unbelievers, provides the foundation for true community among believers. While the world experiences increasing division, God's perfect justice will ultimately restore righteous community in the new heaven and new earth, separating those written in the book of life from those who rejected him.

The prophets of the Old Testament give us even more insight into God's heart for justice. Amos cried out against those who "turn justice into bitterness and cast righteousness to the ground" (Amos 5:7). This shows us that justice should be something sweet and good, not something that leaves a bitter taste in our mouths. Isaiah declared, "Learn to do right; seek justice. Defend the oppressed" (Isaiah 1:17). Notice how he connects doing right with seeking justice— they go hand in hand. Jeremiah spoke against those who "do not promote the case of the fatherless; they do not defend the just cause of the poor" (Jeremiah 5:28). These prophetic voices remind us that justice isn't optional for God's people—it's essential to our faith.

One of the most powerful demonstrations of God's justice is found at the cross of Calvary. Here, we see divine justice and mercy meeting in perfect harmony. The cross shows us that God is so just that sin must be punished, yet so loving that He provided the punishment Himself through His Son. Romans 3:26 confirms this, saying He did it "to demonstrate his righteousness at the present time, so as to be just and the one who justifies those who have faith in Jesus." When we think about justice, we must always view it through the lens of the cross, where God's justice was satisfied not for the sake of punishment alone but also for the sake of reconciliation.

Another powerful example is found in Jesus's encounter with the woman caught in adultery (John 8:1–11). In this situation, Jesus perfectly demonstrated how justice and mercy work together. When the religious leaders brought the woman to Jesus, they were ready to stone her according to the law. Jesus responded by saying, "Let any one of you who is without sin be the first to throw a stone at her" (John 8:7). One by one, they all walked away. Jesus then asked the woman, "Where are they? Has no one condemned you?" (John 8:10). When she said no one had condemned her, Jesus declared, "Then neither do I condemn you. . . . Go now and leave your life of sin"

(John 8:11). He upheld justice by not dismissing her sin, yet showed mercy by not condemning her. This teaches us that just thinking must always be tempered with mercy, which is exactly how God deals with us.

I've experienced this balance of justice and mercy in my own life. During my college years, I made some poor choices that hurt both myself and others. I deserved judgment, but instead, my Christian friends showed me both truth and grace. They didn't ignore my actions or pretend everything was fine—that wouldn't have been just. But they also didn't condemn me—they showed me mercy while helping me understand the importance of making better choices. This experience helped me understand how God's justice and mercy work together in our lives.

Justice isn't just about big moments or dramatic situations; it plays out in our everyday lives in countless small ways:

- How we treat service workers who make mistakes
- The way we handle disputes with neighbors over small issues
- Our responses to family members when they disappoint us
- Our business practices and work ethics, even when no one is watching
- Our use of social media and how we respond to others online

- How we discuss others when they aren't present to defend themselves

I remember a specific situation where I had to practice just thinking in my daily life. I was part of a community project where one team member wasn't pulling their weight. My initial thoughts were judgmental and angry. I wanted to exclude them from our presentation and kick them out of our group. But then I remembered that just thinking requires understanding. When I finally talked with them, I learned they were dealing with work scheduling issues that were affecting their ability to contribute. This taught me that just thinking often requires us to look deeper than surface-level behaviors.

Developing just thoughts requires God's help. We can pray specifically

- for God to reveal any prejudices or biases in our thinking
- for wisdom to see situations from multiple perspectives
- for courage to stand for justice even when it's costly
- for guidance in balancing justice with mercy

One challenge I faced was learning to think justly about myself. When I made mistakes or fell short of my goals, I would often condemn myself harshly. But I've learned that true justice includes accepting

God's forgiveness and extending that same grace to ourselves. This doesn't mean excusing our sins, but it means accepting the justice and mercy that God offers through Christ.

As we think about justice, we look forward to the day when "justice [will roll] on like a river, righteousness like a never-failing stream" (Amos 5:24). Until then, we are called to align our thoughts with God's perfect justice. Every time we choose to think justly about a situation or person, we're participating in God's work of bringing His kingdom values to Earth. When we find ourselves struggling to think justly about others, we can remember that God has shown us perfect justice tempered with mercy through Christ, and we can ask Him to help us show that same combination to others.

My personal experiences have taught me that thinking justly is a daily choice. It's not always easy, and we won't always get it right, but with God's help, we can learn to align our thoughts with His perfect justice. Remember, we're not just called to understand justice but to live it out in our daily thoughts and actions.

As we conclude this exploration of justice, we must remember that living justly isn't just about making fair decisions; it's about embodying God's character in a world desperate for His truth. Through every story shared in this chapter—from the coffee shop scene that opened our discussion to the daily moments of choosing justice over judgment—we've seen how God's perfect justice intersects with our imperfect world.

I was reminded of this truth recently while hearing about a dispute between two church members. Both were convinced they were right, both had valid points, and both wanted justice. As they prayed together and sought God's wisdom, something remarkable happened. The conversation shifted from demanding justice to extending grace, from seeking vindication to pursuing reconciliation. This is the beautiful paradox of biblical justice—it's both uncompromising in its standards and unfathomable in its mercy.

The prophets remind us that justice should "roll down like waters, and righteousness like an everflowing stream" (Amos 5:24 ESV). This imagery suggests that justice isn't stagnant; it's active, powerful, and transformative. Just as a river shapes the landscape it flows through, our commitment to biblical justice should shape every aspect of our lives. It should influence how we treat the cashier who makes a mistake, how we respond to family members who hurt us, how we conduct our business dealings, and how we engage with societal issues.

Remember the God we serve—the One who declared through the prophet Isaiah, "I, the LORD, love justice" (Isaiah 61:8). This isn't a distant, abstract concept. It's the very heart of our Father, displayed most perfectly at the cross where justice and mercy met in divine harmony. When Jesus took the punishment for our sins, He satisfied both God's perfect justice and His infinite love, showing us that true justice always points toward redemption.

As you close this chapter, I challenge you to examine your own heart and actions. Are there areas where you've been quick to judge and slow to understand? Are there situations where God is calling you to stand for justice, even when it's costly? Are there people in your life who need you to extend the same mercy that God has shown you?

Let your prayer be that of David: "Teach me your way, LORD, that I may rely on your faithfulness; give me an undivided heart, that I may fear your name" (Psalm 86:11). Ask God to help you see others through His eyes of justice and mercy. Ask Him for wisdom to know when to stand firm and when to extend grace. Most importantly, ask Him to help you remember that you, too, stand in need of His justice and mercy every day.

In a world where justice often seems elusive, we have the privilege and responsibility of representing God's perfect justice. Not as harsh judges seeking to condemn, but as humble servants seeking to restore. Not as perfect examples, but as forgiven sinners pointing others to the One who is truly just. May we be known not just for what we stand against but for what we stand for—a justice that flows from the heart of God, transforms lives, and points everyone to the hope we have in Christ.

The journey toward just thinking and living is ongoing. Each day presents new opportunities to choose justice over convenience, mercy over judgment, and God's standards over our own preferences.

As we make these choices, we participate in God's work of bringing His kingdom values to Earth. And in doing so, we offer the world a glimpse of the perfect justice that awaits us in eternity—where every wrong will be made right, every tear will be wiped away, and God's justice will reign supreme.

Let us go forward with courage and hope, knowing that even when justice seems distant, we serve a God who promises that it will ultimately prevail. For as the psalmist declared, "The LORD loves righteousness and justice; the earth is full of his unfailing love" (Psalm 33:5). May we be faithful stewards of this divine justice, today and always.

PRACTICE

You just read about how God will make all things right because He is the perfect judge. Even when people hurt us, we are called to forgive and let God take care of the rest. In this practice chapter, write down all the people who have hurt you whom you have not forgiven and why they have hurt you. Whenever you look at the list, pray for them. Prayer is better than judgment. Prayer shows that you love and care. Even though it might be hard to pray, prayer will soften your heart to be able to forgive, and you'll be less likely to judge them in the future.

Just

JOURNAL

4

Pure

THINK

*P*ure is a word that not many people use anymore. When most think of purity, their minds immediately jump to the narrow definition of sexual purity, but the Bible speaks of purity in a much broader and more beautiful sense. God desires us to be pure in mind, heart, and soul—to live with integrity, honesty, and wholesome intentions in every aspect of our lives. He calls us to be free from wicked and impure ways so we can live a holy life that honors Him.

In biblical terms, being pure means striving to align our thoughts and actions with God's perfect will. An impure thought isn't limited to one category; it includes thoughts of dishonesty, hatred, jealousy, revenge, or any behavior that would harm others or ourselves. Let me share with you how we can replace these impure thoughts with what is pure and pleasing to God, and how this transformation can impact every area of our lives.

I want to start by talking about singleness, because this is where many of us begin our journey with purity. Singleness is beautiful! I spent most of my high school and college years single, and while it wasn't always easy, it taught me so much about myself and my relationship with God. The single season can be a rollercoaster of emotions: loneliness, sadness, anger, and jealousy one day; then contentment, joy, and freedom the next. But God has a purpose for every season, including our single years, and these years can be some of the most transformative of our lives if we approach them with the right perspective.

Let me share something personal that really opened my eyes to God's purpose in singleness. During my sophomore year of college, I was constantly praying for a relationship. I'd see couples walking hand in hand across campus and feel this ache in my heart. One particularly lonely Friday night, I decided to skip a party (where all my friends were meeting up with their significant others) and stayed in my dorm room. That night, I opened my Bible randomly and landed on Isaiah 54:5 (ESV): "For your Maker is your husband, the LORD of hosts is his name." Those words hit me like a ton of bricks. I realized I'd been so focused on finding a human relationship that I'd neglected my relationship with God. This moment became a turning point in my spiritual journey.

This revelation completely transformed my perspective on singleness. Instead of seeing it as a waiting period, I began to see it as a gift—a special time to develop my relationship with God without distraction. Jesus Himself was single throughout His earthly ministry, spending His time healing, teaching, and praying.

As Paul writes in 1 Corinthians 7:32–34, "An unmarried man is concerned about the Lord's affairs—how he can please the Lord. But a married man is concerned about the affairs of this world—how he can please his wife—and his interests are divided." This passage took on new meaning as I began to appreciate the unique opportunities that singleness provided for undivided devotion to God.

I'll be completely honest with you—I've had my moments of weakness. There were times when I'd scroll through social media and see all these couples posting their perfect autumn pictures at the pumpkin patch or their romantic beach vacation photos, and my heart would ache with jealousy. But you know what I've learned? Comparison truly is the thief of joy. When we let jealousy creep in, we're essentially telling God that the season He perfectly crafted for us isn't good enough. This realization led me to develop practical strategies for maintaining contentment in my single season.

One strategy that proved particularly helpful was keeping a gratitude journal. Each night, I would write down three things I was thankful for about my current season of life. Sometimes they were big things, like the freedom to spontaneously serve at church events or take mission trips. Other times they were smaller blessings, like being able to eat ice cream for dinner without judgment or having complete control over the TV remote. This practice helped me see the unique blessings that came with my single season.

Let me share a story that really changed my perspective on this. Last summer, I had planned this amazing evening with my best friend: dinner at our favorite restaurant (complete with this potato skin appetizer we'd been craving for weeks), followed by an outdoor movie screening where we'd cozy up in the back of my car with all the blankets and snacks I'd carefully packed. I was so excited about every detail. But when my friend arrived, she immediately started suggesting we do something completely different. My heart sank. That's when God gave me this profound revelation: isn't this exactly what we do to Him when we wish away our current season?

This experience taught me an important lesson about contentment and trust in God's timing. Just as I had carefully planned that evening with my friend, God has carefully planned each season of our lives. When we constantly wish for the next season, we miss the joy and growth opportunities He has placed in our current one. This lesson extends far beyond singleness; it applies to every area of life where we might be tempted to rush ahead of God's perfect timing.

Living in today's world presents unique challenges, especially as a Christian trying to honor God's Word. It feels like everyone else is just looking for temporary connections, while we're seeking something deeper and more meaningful. I remember sitting in my college cafeteria, overhearing conversations about casual relationships and feeling like an alien from another planet because I was committed to waiting for God's best. Sometimes it seems like the concept of purity is completely foreign to our generation.

But here's what I've learned: standing out isn't always a bad thing. In fact, being different often opens doors for meaningful conversations about faith and values. I've had countless opportunities to share my beliefs with curious friends who noticed that I approached relationships differently. These conversations have led to deep discussions about faith, purpose, and the meaning of true love.

Let me tell you about a conversation that really impacted me. I was having coffee with a friend who asked me why I had such high standards for relationships. As I explained my beliefs about waiting for God's timing and maintaining purity in all aspects of life, she started crying. She shared how she wished someone had talked to her about these principles earlier in life. She had experienced so much heartbreak and regret from rushing into relationships without establishing proper foundations. That conversation reminded me why God's standards aren't restrictive; they're protective.

Speaking of protection, let's talk about maintaining purity in all aspects of life. I remember sitting in my high school cafeteria, surrounded by friends who constantly pressured each other to compromise their values. The pressure can feel overwhelming. But I love what Paul writes in 2 Corinthians 12:9: "My grace is sufficient for you, for my power is made perfect in weakness." When we feel like we can't resist temptation on our own, that's exactly where God's strength shines through.

During my junior year, I faced a significant test of my convictions when I became close friends with someone who didn't share my values. While they respected my beliefs on the surface, they often made subtle comments that made me question whether I was being too rigid in my standards. The constant pressure to compromise wore me down, and I found myself starting to question whether I was being too strict. One night, after a particularly challenging conversation about our different viewpoints, I broke down in tears in my car. That's when I felt God's presence so strongly, reminding me that His standards aren't arbitrary; they're designed to protect our hearts, minds, and bodies.

This experience taught me the importance of surrounding myself with friends who share my values and encourage me to grow closer to God. I started being more intentional about my friendships, seeking out mentors who could guide me in my journey, and participating in Bible study groups where I could discuss these challenges openly.

Funny story, one of my mentors was discipling me and a couple other ladies in college, and we were reading through and studying the book of Ruth. This book was tough for me as a single woman in college who just wanted to find a man fit to be her husband. There was a particular day during our discipleship time where I found myself complaining that I was never going to find my Boaz. Little did I know, God had the plan already figured out.

About six months later, I was working a summer job at my college, and there was a single Christian guy, AJ, who was also hired to work there. We started talking and hanging out, but it just so happened that one of his roommates was my mentor's brother-in-law. My mentor was helping her brother-in-law move in and saw AJ reading his Bible in his room. She asked what he was reading, and he said Ruth. My mentor was laughing on the inside because she could see God's plan unfolding right before her eyes. Now AJ is going to be my husband in a few months.

Marriage is talked about a lot in the Bible. God has big expectations for married couples. He cares so much about us that He gives us specific instructions on all things marriage related. He expects the man and women to keep Him at the center of their marriage all the time. Ecclesiastes 4:12 says, "Though one may be overpowered, two can defend themselves. A cord of three strands is not quickly broken." This verse symbolizes the unity between God, a groom, and a bride. When the three stands are braided together, it's harder to break the couple apart. God's love will continue to grow and bind the couple together. I have a lot of mentors in my life who are married, and one thing they all have in common is how they hold each other accountable for spiritual growth. They hold each other up in prayer, encourage reading the Bible, and follow what the Bible says regarding what a marriage is supposed to look like.

However, you might wonder how you can be pure in a marriage. Doesn't purity just get thrown away on your wedding night? No more need to be sexually pure because you are married! Not quite. God desires for all His children to remain pure. In marriage this looks a little different because now you can act on the gift of sex that God has given married people. You must remain pure in your thoughts, though. When you are having sex with your significant other, you shouldn't be thinking about someone else. You should not lust over anyone else but your partner. This is called adultery in the Bible. Adulterers aren't just people who act on their lustful thoughts, but the people who think them too.

Purity isn't just about sex. Purity is about mind and body. I would even argue that purity starts in the mind. Of course, God wants us to stay pure regarding sexual relations until we are married, and there are good reasons for that. Sex is not just a physical act. It is emotionally binding. Have you ever been in or known someone who has been in a relationship where they had sexual relations before marriage? What did you or your friend feel like when you broke up? They were probably heartbroken and devastated. It probably took them longer to heal from that breakup than someone who hadn't had sex. Sex is such an intimate act made for two people who are united as one. It was not created for one-night stands.

I love sharing this beautiful analogy I learned from *Jane the Virgin* (one of my favorite shows!). One day,

Jane's grandma handed her a perfect rose and asked her to admire its beauty. Then she told her to crush it in her hands. When Jane did, her grandma asked her to make it look perfect again. Of course, she couldn't. "This," she said, "is why we protect what's precious." While this analogy is often used to address physical purity, it applies to all forms of purity—our thoughts, our words, our actions. Everything precious in life requires protection and care.

Building on Jane's grandmother's wisdom, I've learned that purity extends to every aspect of our lives. It's about maintaining integrity in our work, being honest in our relationships, and staying true to our values even when no one is watching. It's about the media we consume, the conversations we engage in, and the way we treat others. Every choice we make either strengthens or weakens our commitment to living a pure life.

One area where this particularly applies is our use of social media. In our digital age, maintaining purity of mind and heart has become increasingly challenging. I had to unfollow several accounts that, while not explicitly inappropriate, were causing me to compare myself to unrealistic standards or triggering unhealthy thoughts. Proverbs 4:23 tells us to guard our hearts, for everything we do flows from it. Sometimes that means making tough decisions about what we allow into our minds through our screens.

I remember struggling with this during my freshman year. I followed several influencers for "motivation," but their posts were actually feeding my insecurities and leading to unhealthy behaviors. It took a heart-to-heart conversation with my small group leader to help me see how these seemingly innocent follows were affecting my mental purity and self-image. She reminded me that guarding our purity sometimes means cutting off things that might seem harmless but are actually hindering our spiritual growth.

This led me to develop what I call my "digital purity plan." I set specific boundaries around my social media use, including designated phone-free times each day, regular digital fasts, and careful curation of my feed to ensure it aligns with my values. I also started following accounts that encouraged my faith and personal growth rather than those that triggered comparison or discontent.

Purity of speech is another aspect we don't talk about enough. James 3:9–10 points out how we praise God with our mouths and then turn around and curse people made in His image. I've caught myself participating in gossip under the guise of "sharing prayer requests" or making cutting remarks about others' choices. God convicted me that these behaviors were just as much a purity issue as any other area of life.

To address this, I started practicing what I call the "three-filter test" before speaking: Is it true? Is it kind? Is it necessary? This simple practice has transformed the way I communicate and has helped me maintain purity in my speech. It's amazing how many potential comments don't make it past these three simple questions!

The battle for purity ultimately takes place in our minds. Romans 12:2 tells us not to conform to the pattern of this world but to be transformed by the renewing of our minds. This transformation isn't a one-time event; it's a daily choice to filter our thoughts through God's truth. When impure thoughts come (and they will), we have the power through Christ to take them captive (2 Corinthians 10:5).

Being biblically pure in mind generally refers to having thoughts and attitudes that align with the teachings and values found in the Bible. This includes having a mind-set characterized by virtues such as love, humility, honesty, kindness, and purity. It involves avoiding sinful thoughts and behaviors, and instead focusing on thoughts that are righteous and honor God.

If your mind is not pure and if your thoughts are not focused on God, your actions and words become impure. An impure mind can look like many things, but here are some specific examples:

1. Obsessive thoughts—Constantly dwelling on negative or harmful ideas, such as revenge or hatred toward others.
2. Addictive behaviors—Being consumed by addictions like drugs, alcohol, gambling, or even excessive consumption of media that promotes negativity.

3. Dishonesty—Habitual lying or deceitfulness, whether to oneself or others, which can cloud judgment and lead to further moral compromises.

4. Prejudice and bigotry—Holding prejudiced views toward certain groups of people based on race, religion, gender, or other factors, leading to discriminatory thoughts and behaviors.

5. Manipulative tendencies—Using others for personal gain without regard for their well-being, often through deceit or emotional manipulation.

6. Violent fantasies—Regularly imagining or planning violent acts against others, even if they are not acted upon, which can indicate a deeply troubled mind.

7. Selfishness and greed—Constantly putting one's own desires and needs above those of others, without consideration for fairness or justice.

8. Inappropriate sexual thoughts—Fixating on sexual fantasies or behaviors that are harmful or exploitative, disregarding consent and respect for others.

9. Resentment and bitterness—Holding on to grudges or feelings of bitterness toward others, which can poison relationships and one's outlook on life.

10. Lack of empathy—Being unable or unwilling to understand or share the feelings of others, leading to callous or insensitive behavior.

To be biblically pure in mind means striving to think in ways that are consistent with the principles and commandments outlined in the Bible. This often involves prayer, meditation on Scripture, and seeking guidance from the Holy Spirit to help maintain a pure and holy thought life. It's about cultivating a mind-set that reflects the character of Christ and seeking to glorify God in all aspects of one's thinking and attitudes.

It's important to note that if you have any impure thoughts, you are not the only one. Most people struggle with them, and it's because of the Enemy. Satan is very sneaky, and if he can get you to look at an everyday object or another person and cause you to think badly about it or them, then he is halfway to winning over your mind. You see, Satan does not know what you are thinking. He is not a mind reader. Only God knows our thoughts. However, if you have these thoughts and they ruminate inside you, they will eventually come out in the form of sin. And sin separates us from God. And that is what Satan wants.

God, on the other hand, wants us to remain pure and keep our eyes on Him because in Him are all good things. The sin that Satan wants you to participate in might fulfill you for a minute or maybe even a week, but after that you'll just be wanting more, and it will end up being a vicious cycle. God is willing to sustain you so you never have to be in that cycle again.

Last year I started keeping a "purity journal" where I write down scriptures about purity and log my struggles and victories in this area. It's been incredible to see how God has been faithful in helping me overcome patterns of impure thinking. One entry that particularly stands out was from a day when I was feeling overwhelmed by temptation. I wrote down Psalm 51:10: "Create in me a pure heart, O God, and renew a steadfast spirit within me." That simple prayer became my anchor during a difficult season.

Through this journaling practice, I've also documented the many ways God has provided strength in moments of weakness. Each entry serves as a reminder of His faithfulness and helps me track my growth in different areas of purity. It's encouraging to look back and see how far God has brought me, even in areas where I once struggled intensely.

Remember, pursuing purity isn't about following a list of rules or trying to earn God's love. It's about living in a way that honors Him because we love Him. When we understand that we are His temple (1 Corinthians 6:19–20), purity becomes less about restriction and more about protection. We protect what's valuable, and you, my friend, are priceless to God.

This journey of pursuing purity has taught me so much about God's character and His love for us. Each time I choose to honor Him with my thoughts, words, and actions, I grow closer to Him and understand more deeply why His ways are perfect. The temporary pleasures of compromise pale in comparison to the joy of walking in step with our Creator.

Purity flows from having a heart surrendered to God. So let's summarize the main areas of purity we are called to.

Purity of heart involves cultivating a deep relationship with God through prayer, meditation on His Word, and obedience to His commands. It requires honesty with ourselves and with God, acknowledging our weaknesses and relying on His strength to overcome temptations. Living with a pure heart enables us to love others genuinely, serve selflessly, and worship God authentically, reflecting His character in all we do.

Purity of heart, as described by Jesus in the Beatitudes (Matthew 5:8), goes beyond mere external actions; it speaks to the core of our being. The heart, in biblical terms, represents the seat of our emotions, thoughts, and intentions. Jesus teaches that those who are pure in heart are blessed because they will see God. This purity involves integrity and sincerity in our motives, aligning our desires with God's will.

In a world where external appearances often take precedence, Jesus emphasizes the internal condition of the heart. This purity requires us to examine our motivations and attitudes, seeking to rid ourselves of selfish ambitions, deceitful desires, and prideful thoughts. It entails surrendering our hearts fully to God, allowing Him to purify and transform us from within (Psalm 51:10).

Sexual purity involves abstaining from all forms of sexual activity outside marriage, as defined by God's design (Hebrews 13:4). It includes avoiding pornography, lustful thoughts, masturbation, and any behavior that objectifies or exploits others. Our bodies, created in the image of God, are to be respected and treated with dignity, not used for selfish gratification or sinful indulgence. This includes dressing modestly.

In 1 Corinthians 6:18–20, Paul addresses the importance of sexual purity, urging believers to flee from sexual immorality because our bodies are temples of the Holy Spirit. This aspect of purity encompasses the physical aspect of our beings—using our bodies in ways that honor God.

Living a life of sexual purity requires discipline, self-control, and a commitment to biblical standards in a culture that often promotes promiscuity and moral relativism. It necessitates guarding our minds and hearts, setting boundaries in relationships, and seeking accountability and support from fellow believers. Sexual purity is not just about behavior but also about cultivating a mind-set and lifestyle that honors God's gift of sexuality within the context of marriage.

Let's talk a bit more about our bodies as temples of the Holy Spirit. We need to treat our bodies like the gift they are, and I know so often it's hard—especially for women—to take care of it accordingly. We should not be overindulging in food, overexercising, undereating, or picking ourselves apart with things we want to change.

Purity of speech involves being mindful of our words, speaking with kindness and humility, and considering the impact of our communication on others.

It requires listening attentively, seeking understanding before responding, and using our words to build bridges rather than barriers. Honoring God with our speech involves aligning our words with His Word, speaking truth in love, and being a source of encouragement and edification to those around us.

Ephesians 4:29 challenges believers to guard their speech, ensuring that only words that build others up and benefit those who listen are spoken. Purity of speech involves the words we use, the tone we adopt, and the attitudes we convey through our communication.

Our words have the power to uplift and encourage or to tear down and destroy (Proverbs 18:21). Purity of speech requires us to refrain from gossip, slander, profanity, and any form of unwholesome talk that dishonors God and hurts others. Instead, our speech should be seasoned with grace, reflecting the love and truth of Christ (Colossians 4:6).

Purity in worship means participating in corporate worship with a heart of gratitude and humility, lifting our voices in praise and worship with sincerity and fervor. It involves engaging in prayer, meditation on Scripture, and communion with God, allowing His Spirit to guide and transform our worship experience. Purity in worship enables us to encounter God's presence, experience His peace and joy, and grow in intimacy with Him, both individually and as part of a faith community.

Psalm 24:3–4 poses a question about who may ascend to God's holy place, emphasizing the necessity of clean hands and a pure heart. Purity in worship involves approaching God with reverence, sincerity, and a desire to honor Him in every aspect of our worship experience.

Worship is more than ritual or routine; it is a life-style characterized by devotion and adoration of God. Purity in worship requires authenticity and transparency before God, acknowledging our sins and seeking His forgiveness and cleansing (1 John 1:9). It involves offering ourselves as living sacrifices, holy and pleasing to God, as an act of spiritual worship (Romans 12:1).

Purity in relationships means honoring commitments, speaking truth in love, and resolving conflicts biblically and peacefully (Matthew 18:15–17). It requires humility to admit faults, forgiveness to reconcile differences, and grace to extend mercy and compassion to others. Purity in relationships also includes guarding our hearts against unhealthy attachments, maintaining appropriate boundaries, and seeking God's guidance in forming and nurturing meaningful connections that honor Him.

First Timothy 5:22 gives us practical wisdom for our relationships: "Do not be hasty in the laying on of hands, and do not share in the sins of others. Keep yourself pure." This verse cautions us against rushing to appoint leaders without proper vetting, which could lead to problems later. It also warns us to be careful about who we closely associate with, as we can easily be pulled into others' sinful behaviors. At its heart, the verse calls us to maintain personal purity in all our interactions. When we approach relationships with integrity, respect, and genuine love, we protect both ourselves and our community from the damage that comes from hasty decisions and compromised standards.

Our relationships should reflect God's love and grace, fostering unity, mutual encouragement, and accountability within the body of Christ. This purity involves avoiding gossip, bitterness, deceit, and any behavior that damages or undermines the trust and harmony essential for healthy relationships.

Purity as holiness means seeking to please God in every thought, word, and deed, seeking His kingdom above all else (Matthew 6:33). It involves cultivating a lifestyle of worship, prayer, and obedience to God's Word, allowing His truth to renew our minds and hearts continually. Holiness empowers us to be effective witnesses for Christ, shining His light in a dark world and reflecting His love and grace to others.

Leviticus 11:44–45 and 1 Peter 1:15–16 emphasize God's call for His people to be holy as He is holy, encompassing both moral purity and separation from sin. Holiness is the overarching principle that governs every aspect of purity discussed above—it is the state of being set apart for God's purposes and reflecting His character in all areas of life.

Living a life of holiness and purity requires intentional choices and daily surrender to God's will and Word. It involves renouncing worldly desires and conforming to God's standards of righteousness and truth (Romans 12:2). Holiness is not achieved through our own efforts but through the transforming work of the Holy Spirit within us, enabling us to live in obedience and faithfulness to God.

Purity as outlined in Scripture encompasses the entirety of our lives—our hearts, bodies, speech, worship, relationships, and pursuit of holiness. It is a journey of faith and obedience, enabled by the Holy Spirit, to live in accordance with God's will and reflect His glory to the world. May we continually seek God's grace and strength to pursue purity in every aspect of our lives, knowing that He who calls us is faithful to complete the work He has begun in us (Philippians 1:6).

I want to end this chapter by sharing a truth that transformed my understanding of purity. During a particularly challenging season, my mentor shared Psalm 84:11 with me: "No good thing does he withhold from those whose walk is blameless." She helped me see that God's standards for purity aren't about keeping good things from us; they're about preparing us for the best things He has planned.

This verse has become my go-to reminder when temptation strikes or when I'm tempted to compromise my standards. I remember that God isn't a cosmic killjoy trying to restrict my happiness. He's a loving Father who wants to protect me and prepare me for His best. Every "no" to impurity is actually a "yes" to something better.

Whether you're single, dating, or married, remember that the pursuit of purity is a journey, not a destination. There will be struggles and setbacks, but God's grace is sufficient. He sees your heart's desire to honor Him, and He is faithful to provide the strength you need. Keep fighting the good fight, dear friend. The reward of a pure heart far outweighs any temporary pleasure this world can offer.

As you continue on your journey, remember that you're not alone. Surround yourself with people who share your values and will encourage you in your pursuit of purity. Find a mentor who can guide you, join a Bible study group where you can discuss these challenges openly, and most importantly, stay connected to God through regular prayer and Bible study. He is faithful to complete the good work He has begun in you.

PRACTICE

In Philippians 4:8, Paul encourages us to think on things that are pure, lovely, admirable, and praiseworthy. But how often do we really stop to consider what we allow to enter and dwell in our minds? Our thoughts shape our actions, our attitudes, and ultimately, our character. A mind that focuses on purity can transform the way we live, but to start, we need to be aware of what's already going on in our thought life.

That's where the Thought Inventory comes in.

This exercise will help you recognize patterns in your thinking. Over the next seven days, I want to challenge you to write down your thoughts throughout the day. Don't edit them or try to make them look better than they are—just capture them honestly. At the end of each day, take time to review and reflect on what you wrote. Were your thoughts aligned with purity, or did you notice some areas where they strayed into negativity, criticism, or impurity? This inventory will help you spot where you need to invite God's transforming power into your mind.

HOW TO TAKE A THOUGHT INVENTORY

1. Set an Intention
   - Each morning, ask God to help you be aware of your thoughts. Pray for the ability to notice them without judgment and for the courage to change what's not aligned with His will.

2. Capture Your Thoughts
   • Throughout the day, whenever you can, jot down what's on your mind. You can use your phone, a notebook, or even sticky notes. Aim for capturing at least ten different thoughts each day, though you might notice more. Here are a few examples:
     ▪ *I'm so frustrated with my coworker right now.*
     ▪ *I don't know if I'll ever be good enough for this job.*
     ▪ *I'm really thankful for the way that situation worked out.*

3. Reflect Daily
   • At the end of each day, set aside ten to fifteen minutes to review your thoughts. Use the following questions to guide your reflection:
     ▪ Did my thoughts reflect purity, goodness, and truth today?
     ▪ Were there any thoughts that were impure, negative, or harmful to myself or others?
     ▪ How much time did I spend dwelling on these negative or impure thoughts?
     ▪ How did my thoughts affect my mood, behavior, or interactions with others?

4. Identify Patterns
   • By the end of the week, you'll likely notice patterns. Do certain people, situations, or environments trigger impure or negative thoughts?

Are there times of day when you're more prone to struggling with your thoughts? Identifying these patterns is the first step toward renewing your mind (Romans 12:2).

5. Bring It to God
   • After completing your inventory, bring your findings to God in prayer. Confess any thoughts that are not pleasing to Him, and ask for help in redirecting your mind toward purity. Remember, transformation begins with awareness, but true renewal comes through the Holy Spirit.

Example Thought Inventory:

Date	Thought	Pure/ Impure/ Neutral	Notes
Monday, 9:00 a.m.	*I can't believe how rude they were to me.*	Impure	Dwelling on anger for too long
Monday, 1:00 p.m.	*I'm grateful for a quiet lunch break.*	Pure	Feeling thankful and peaceful
Monday, 5:00 p.m.	*I'll never finish this project in time.*	Impure	Anxiety over deadlines, needs faith and focus

Use this exercise to become more intentional about what fills your mind. Over time, you'll find that as you become more aware of your thoughts, it will be easier to redirect them toward what is pure and lovely.

Pure

JOURNAL

5

Lovely

THINK

When I think of the word *lovely*, do you know what first comes to my mind? Sunrises and sunsets. They always take my breath away, and I am left in awe by the artistry. Every single sunset and sunrise is different, painting the sky with unique combinations of colors that will never be exactly replicated again. Standing on my balcony last week, I watched as the sky transformed from soft pink to brilliant orange to deep purple, each moment more breathtaking than the last. It reminded me of how God creates these masterpieces twice daily, yet we often rush past them without a second glance.

The science behind these daily displays of beauty is fascinating. The vibrant colors we see during sunrises and sunsets are due to the scattering of light in the earth's atmosphere. Shorter wavelengths of light like blue and violet are scattered more strongly by air molecules and particles, leaving longer wavelengths like red, orange, and yellow to dominate the sky. What's even more amazing is that sunsets are actually an illusion. What we see in the sky is just the refraction of the sun—by the time we perceive those brilliant colors, the sun has already dipped below the horizon. The earth's atmosphere bends the sunlight, allowing us to witness this daily miracle.

This scientific understanding doesn't diminish the wonder; if anything, it deepens it. Last night, as I watched the sunset with my pastor's young daughter, she asked me why the sky turns pink. As I explained the basic concept of light scattering, her eyes widened with wonder. "So God made the air just right to paint pictures for us?" she asked. Her childlike perspective reminded me that sometimes the most profound truths come from the simplest observations.

But beyond the scientific explanation, these celestial displays speak to something deeper in my soul. When I see a sunrise, I'm reminded of new beginnings, hope, and renewal. Each morning brings fresh mercy and another chance to start anew. Sunsets, on the other hand, remind me that endings can be beautiful too. Just last month, I was struggling with the end of a long-term friendship. Watching a particularly stunning sunset, I felt God reminding me that even life's endings can hold their own kind of beauty and purpose.

Creation's loveliness extends far beyond just the sky. There are countless examples of gorgeous phenomena in our world, and chances are, each of those things is highly complex. What we see with our eyes is the raw beauty, but underneath lies a whole network of science and layers upon layers of God's artistry. Take the butterfly I saw in the community garden yesterday—its wings were a stunning array of blue and black, but beneath that visible beauty lies an intricate system of scales, each one precisely positioned to create both color and functionality.

Speaking of gardens, my grandma and grandpa's garden has become a sanctuary of sorts, a place where I've learned to slow down and notice God's intricate design. This spring, they decided to plant a wildflower meadow in the corner that used to be just plain grass. The transformation has been remarkable. Now, instead of a uniform green rectangle, they have a vibrant tapestry of colors and textures that changes almost daily. Purple coneflowers dance with yellow black-eyed Susans, while delicate Queen Anne's lace adds its lacy white touches throughout. The variety of pollinators it has attracted is stunning—not just butterflies, but native bees, hummingbirds, and even the occasional hummingbird moth, which looks like a magical creature hovering in the twilight.

I need to be personal here because I know many people struggle with this too. I get caught up in the busyness of life. More often than not, I'm searching for something to do and don't allow myself any downtime. During college, I was addicted to the rush. My schedule was packed from the moment I woke up until I collapsed into bed at night. Classes, study groups, club meetings, work study, volunteer commitments—I tried to do it all. The days were a blur, and I hate to admit this, but I feel like I missed out on some precious memories because of that constant rush.

That rushed lifestyle didn't end with graduation either. If anything, entering the professional world only intensified it. Although my job was less demanding and less busy than college, I still found myself looking for opportunities to stay busy. I found myself taking classes to become a personal trainer and nutritionist, looking for part-time jobs, and constantly thinking about the next project. The world seemed to reward this behavior—my LinkedIn followers praised my "dedication," and I quickly earned a reputation as someone who could be counted on to get things done.

Last week, I found my old college planner while cleaning out my closet. Looking through those packed pages, I remembered how I thought I always had to do more to get the most out of my college experience. Now, looking back, I realize I never took the time to recognize the beauty around me. Every day, I had the chance to get to know my classmates better, to have meaningful conversations over meals with my best friends, to connect more deeply with professors and mentors, or to simply sit by the campus fountain and appreciate the moment. But I failed to see the loveliness in those opportunities. While I did earn awards and maintain a perfect GPA, I failed to breathe and meditate on the loveliness of God and what He had placed all around me.

The turning point came during a particularly hectic period at college when I worked on campus. I was managing three major projects simultaneously, barely sleeping, and running my body ragged (literally).

One morning, as I rushed to an early meeting on campus, I literally ran into a professor who was slowly walking through the campus. As I hurriedly apologized, she smiled and said, "Why don't you join me for a moment? The morning light on the fountain in the middle of campus is especially beautiful today." Something in her peaceful demeanor made me pause. I glanced at my watch, then at my phone full of unread messages, and then at the gentle ripples on the fountain's surface, golden in the morning light. For the first time in months, I chose beauty over busyness.

This morning, I made a conscious effort to slow down. Instead of immediately checking my phone when I woke up, I sat outside with my hot tea and simply listened to the birds singing their morning songs. It struck me how often we go through life without even looking twice at the nature around us. We're too busy to enjoy these small daily concerts. We fail to look up at the stars at night, too preoccupied with our screens or our worries about tomorrow. We work and work but don't recognize our Creator's work all around us.

That morning silence revealed something else, too—the sound of my own breathing, the gentle rhythm of life itself. In those quiet moments, I began to notice things I'd overlooked before: the way the morning dew caught the light like scattered diamonds on the grass, the intricate pattern of veins in a fallen leaf, the methodical way a spider repaired its web. Each observation felt like a small gift, a reminder of the countless beautiful details woven into the fabric of creation.

And it's not just nature I'm talking about. Do you know what God's most lovely creation is? You. And me. And the person next to you. And your coworker. And yes, even your nemesis. And your ex-boyfriend. And your stepfather. You get the point. Humans are God's most prized, lovely creation. You are lovely. This truth hit me particularly hard last week when I was struggling with self-image issues. Looking in the mirror, all I could see were flaws, but then I remembered that I was criticizing God's handiwork.

This reminds me of a conversation I had with my teenage youth group girls recently. One girl was showing me social media filters that could completely transform her appearance—smoothing her skin, enlarging her eyes, even reshaping her face. "Isn't it cool?" she asked, but I could hear the underlying uncertainty in all of their voices. We spent the next hour talking about true beauty, about how God deliberately chose every feature of her face, every curl in her hair. We talked about how society's standards of beauty are constantly changing, but God's view of our loveliness never wavers.

Let me return to sunsets and sunrises for a moment. I know some might not believe me when I say this, but you are more beautiful than the skies. Sometimes, okay maybe most of the time, it's hard for me to accept a compliment. When my fiancé says, "You are so beautiful" or "You are drop-dead gorgeous," I struggle to

Whatever Is

simply say thank you. But think about this: when you're at the beach looking at a sunset, it's so beautiful that you immediately want to capture it, right? Like most people, I take pictures of every sunset I see. But when you look at the picture later, it never quite captures the true beauty of what you witnessed in person.

The same principle applies to the moments when we feel most alive, most ourselves. Last weekend, I attended a friend's wedding. During the reception, the photographer captured a moment when I was laughing with old friends, completely unaware of the camera. When I saw the photo later, I barely recognized myself— not because I looked different but because the joy radiating from my face was so pure and unfiltered. It wasn't a posed smile or a carefully arranged expression; it was just me, fully present in a moment of genuine happiness.

It's the same with us. If you've ever seen a picture of yourself that you absolutely don't like, it might trigger negative emotions about your appearance. But you're not the one seeing yourself laughing with friends, doing a hobby, or hanging out with your family. Other people see your loveliness in ways you might miss. Just yesterday, a friend showed me a candid photo she'd taken of me while I was teaching Sunday school. While I initially focused on my awkward pose, she pointed out the joy radiating from my face as I interacted with the children. Sometimes it's hard to notice our own beauty, especially if we already have an ingrained negative image in our head.

This reminds me of a powerful moment I witnessed at a women's retreat I attended in high school. We did an exercise where each person had to write down three things they loved about their appearance. The room grew quiet as women struggled with this seemingly simple task. Then we passed our papers to the person on our right, and they had to add three more beautiful things they noticed about us. By the time the papers made it around the circle, each woman held a list of dozens of lovely attributes about herself—seen through the eyes of others. There were tears, hugs, and breakthrough moments as women began to see themselves as others saw them, as God sees them.

Take on your identity as a child of the King, and don't forget that He made you lovely. You are His most prized creation. Last Sunday, our pastor asked a profound question that has stuck with me all week: "Would you want to criticize the work of the greatest Artist to ever exist?"

That question led me to reflect on how we often treat ourselves and others. Would we speak about a masterpiece painting the way we sometimes speak to ourselves? Would we look at a sunset and point out its flaws? Of course not! Yet we readily criticize ourselves, God's masterpieces, without a second thought. This weekend, I'm leading a youth group discussion about identity, and I plan to use this analogy to help them understand their worth in God's eyes.

What I think Paul was really emphasizing in Philippians 4:8 is the importance of focusing on God's goodness and grace. We need to meditate on the love-liness of how good our God is and how His grace never ends. Just this morning, I was journaling about all the ways God demonstrates His goodness in our lives. He gives us eyes to see the beautiful world around us. He gives us ears to hear the melodies and rhythms of a bird's song or of our mothers singing a lullaby. He gives us nerves in our bodies so we can feel even the most intimate touch and experience the world around us through physical sensation. He gifted us with taste buds so we can enjoy the foods He placed on this earth to nourish our bodies.

And speaking of physical senses, I've been learning to appreciate them more intentionally lately. This morning, I took a "sensory walk" through my neigh-borhood, deliberately focusing on one sense at a time. First, I just listened—to leaves rustling, distant traffic, children playing, a dog barking. Then I focused on what I could see—the play of light and shadow, the various shades of green in different plants, the architec-tural details of houses I pass every day but never really notice. Next came smell—someone's fresh laundry, blooming jasmine, the earthy scent after a brief rain shower. Even touch became a source of wonder—the different textures of tree bark, the smooth coolness of a stone wall, the gentle brush of wind on my skin.

Last night, I was cooking dinner, using fresh herbs from a friend's garden. As I chopped basil and rose-mary, the aromatic scents filled the kitchen, and I was struck by how God didn't just make food nutritious;

He made it delicious and appealing to our senses. He cares about us so deeply, and we don't deserve that care. We are sinful, but He decided to have mercy on us and extend His loving grace. He gave us what we don't deserve—a relationship with Him and an opportunity to live this lovely life and glorify Him with it.

The kitchen has become one of my favorite places to experience God's lovely gifts. There's something almost sacred about the process of preparing food—the way simple ingredients combine to create something new and wonderful, the way flavors and textures work together in harmony. In college, when I was a Fellowship of Christian Athletes leader, I hosted a program that included dinner parties where everyone brought a dish that reminded them of God's goodness. The stories shared around that table were as nourishing as the food itself—tales of family traditions, childhood memories, and moments when God's presence was felt through something as simple as Grandma's apple pie or Dad's famous chili.

Have you ever read the book of Song of Solomon in the Bible? Well, if you haven't, it is quite the read. This book is a poem about two lovers, a bride and a groom. It also has a deeper meaning as an allegory of God's love for His people. While reading it, you might become uncomfortable during some of the verses. However, it is a beautiful expression of love and admiration, describing the beauty and loveliness of the beloved.

What strikes me most about Song of Solomon is its unapologetic celebration of human love and beauty.

In a world that often either sensationalizes, stigma-tizes, or oversexualizes romance, this book pres-ents a balanced, God-honoring view of love in all its dimensions. It reminds us that our capacity for deep, passionate love is itself a reflection of God's image in us. When I lead young adult Bible studies, this book often generates the most interesting discussions about God's design for love and relationship.

Last month during my quiet time, I was particu-larly moved by Song of Solomon 2:10–12 (ESV): "My beloved speaks and says to me: 'Arise, my love, my beautiful one, and come away, for behold, the winter is past; the rain is over and gone. The flowers appear on the earth, the time of singing has come, and the voice of the turtledove is heard in our land.'" Reading these words as if they were God speaking directly to me to share with a family member of mine brought tears to my eyes.

I experienced the truth of these verses in a powerful way when one of my close family members was in a period of depression. For months, everything had felt dark and heavy for them, like an endless winter of the soul. But gradually, through the support of their church community and the gentle presence of God, spring began to return. First in small ways—a genuine laugh here, a moment of peace there. Then in larger ways—the return of hope, the ability to see beauty again, the renewal of joy in worship. God was calling this family member to arise, to come away from the winter season, to embrace the new life He was offering.

Another verse that never fails to move me is Song of Solomon 4:7 (ESV): "You are altogether beautiful, my love; there is no flaw in you." In a world that constantly points out our imperfections, these words remind us how God sees us through the lens of His perfect love.

This verse has become especially meaningful in my ministry to women struggling with eating disorders and body image issues. Recently, I started a support group online where we focus on seeing ourselves as God sees us. Each week, we study different scriptures about God's love and our identity in Christ. The transformation in these women's lives as they begin to internalize God's truth about their worth and beauty is nothing short of miraculous.

But perhaps the most powerful passage is found in Song of Solomon 8:6–7 (ESV): "Set me as a seal upon your heart, as a seal upon your arm, for love is strong as death, jealousy is fierce as the grave. Its flashes are flashes of fire, the very flame of the LORD. Many waters cannot quench love, neither can floods drown it." When I read these verses again, imagining them as God speaking to me in a love letter, they take on an even deeper meaning.

These verses speak to the unshakeable nature of God's love—a truth I've experienced personally through some of life's deepest valleys. Thirteen years ago, when my parents got a divorce, I struggled to feel God's presence in the midst of our family's pain. But even in the darkest moments of that journey, His love remained constant. Like a seal upon my heart, it couldn't be washed away by tears or drowned by fear. Through every counseling session, every sleepless night, every moment of uncertainty, God's love was our anchor.

The line that really resonates with me is that "many waters cannot quench love, neither can floods drown it." Just last week, I was feeling particularly unlovable after making a series of mistakes at work. But even in those moments of self-doubt and disappointment, God's love remained steadfast—like those powerful waves I witnessed in Ireland during my study abroad trip. Speaking of lovely things, I have to share one of the most breathtaking experiences of my life. On the final day of our time in Ireland, our group ventured off the beaten path to a hidden cliff overlooking the Atlantic Ocean. What we discovered there left me speechless.

The landscape before us was almost otherworldly in its beauty. Rolling hills, covered in grass so vibrantly green it seemed almost impossible, stretched out to meet dramatic cliffs that dropped away to the churning sea below. As the sun began its descent, the sky painted itself in brilliant streaks of gold and pink, while waves crashed against the ancient rocks below, sending spray high into the air. In that moment, standing on the edge of that Irish cliff, I felt smaller yet somehow more significant than ever before—a tiny part of God's magnificent creation, yet deeply loved by the Artist who crafted it all.

That evening in Ireland taught me something profound about loveliness. Sometimes the most beautiful things aren't the obvious tourist attractions or the carefully curated Instagram spots; they're the unexpected moments when God reveals His artistry in ways that take our breath away. The untamed power of those waves, the impossible softness of the grass beneath my feet, the wild beauty of that unspoiled coastline—it all spoke of a Creator who delights in both grandeur and detail.

This brings me back to Paul's words about dwelling on whatever is lovely. When we train our hearts to notice beauty—whether it's in a dramatic Irish sunset, during a quiet morning in our own backyard, or in the face of someone we love—we're actually practicing a form of worship. We're acknowledging the Master Artist and allowing ourselves to be transformed by the recognition of His handiwork all around us.

So maybe that's the real secret to living a life focused on loveliness—it's not about seeking out perfect moments or Instagram-worthy scenes. It's about developing eyes that see God's beauty in both the extraordinary and the ordinary. It's about slowing down enough to notice the way light plays on water, the sound of children's laughter, the warmth of a friend's smile. It's about recognizing that we ourselves are part of that beauty, carefully crafted by a loving Creator who delights in making all things lovely.

And when we struggle to see that loveliness—in ourselves, in others, or in the world around us—we can remember that God's love, like those powerful Irish waves, cannot be quenched. It continues to shape us, to mold us, and to reveal its beauty in unexpected ways. We just need to pause long enough to notice it.

PRACTICE

Write down all the things that come to your mind that you think are lovely. This can include people, nature, acts, architecture, animals, or anything else you can think of.

Now write why you think these things are lovely.

Now write a love letter to yourself.

Lastly, write a love letter to the Creator of all lovely things.

JOURNAL

6

Commendable

THINK

*W*hen we hear the word *commendable*, it means something or someone worthy of praise and admiration, someone we look up to or respect. As we look around, we might see examples of people we admire: athletes who work hard and inspire us, musicians who create beautiful songs, or even close friends or family members who are kind and loving. But no matter how amazing these people are, there's someone far more worthy of our praise—God. When we take time to really think about who God is and what He's done, we realize there's no one more commendable than Him.

Let's dive into why God is so worthy of praise, looking at the incredible ways He's shown us His power, love, faithfulness, forgiveness, and perfect plans through both His Word and our lives.

We all know someone who's really good at something—maybe your friend can solve a Rubik's Cube in seconds or your dad can fix anything that's broken. But no matter how talented or powerful someone might seem, their abilities are nothing compared to

God's power. The Bible shows us over and over again just how powerful God is, and that's one of the reasons why He's so worthy of praise.

Let's start at the very beginning. Genesis 1 tells us that God created everything simply by speaking it into existence. Can you imagine? He said, "Let there be light," and suddenly there was light! He made the sky, the sea, the land, the plants, and every living thing just by His words. Psalm 33:6 says, "By the word of the Lord the heavens were made, their starry host by the breath of His mouth." God didn't need to gather supplies or spend days working; He spoke, and it happened.

One of my favorite stories that shows God's power is the story of Moses and the Red Sea in Exodus 14. The Israelites were escaping Egypt, but they were trapped between the Red Sea in front of them and Pharaoh's army chasing from behind. It seemed impossible for them to escape. But God told Moses to lift his staff over the sea, and when he did, God parted the waters! The people walked through on dry ground, and when the Egyptians tried to follow, the waters came crashing down. That's how powerful our God is—He can even control the sea! God's power is unmatched, and that alone makes Him worthy of praise.

Another thing that makes God so praiseworthy is His incredible love. Unlike human love, which can sometimes be selfish or conditional, God's love is perfect. It doesn't change based on how well we perform, how much we pray, or whether we always make the right choices. God loves us because that's who He is.

We see this most clearly in the life and death of Jesus. John 3:16 says, "For God so loved the world that he gave his one and only Son, that whoever believes in him shall not perish but have eternal life." Think about that for a minute. God loves us so much that He was willing to send His only Son to die for us so that we could be saved. Jesus came to Earth, lived a perfect life, and died on the cross to take the punishment for our sins. And then He rose again, conquering death so we could have eternal life with Him.

One story that shows God's love in action is the story of the prodigal son in Luke 15. In the story, a son asks his father for his inheritance early, which is like saying, "I don't care about you; I just want your money." He takes the money, runs away, and wastes it all on wild living. When he's out of money and desperate, he decides to return home, hoping his father will at least hire him as a servant. But when he returns, his father runs to meet him, wraps him in a hug, and throws a huge party to celebrate his return. That's a picture of God's love for us. Even when we mess up, God is waiting with open arms to welcome us back. His love is unconditional and endless.

One of the most comforting things about God is that He never changes. While people might let us down or circumstances might shift, God remains the same yesterday, today, and forever (Hebrews 13:8). This is why we can trust Him completely—He never breaks His promises. His faithfulness is commendable because we know that no matter what happens, we can count on Him.

We see an example of God's faithfulness in the story of Abraham and Sarah. In Genesis 12, God promised Abraham that he would be the father of a great nation, even though Abraham and his wife, Sarah, didn't have any children and were well beyond the age of having kids. It seemed impossible. But God is always faithful to His promises. When Abraham was a hundred years old, God gave them a son, Isaac, fulfilling His promise. It didn't happen in the timing Abraham expected, but God never failed him. And just as He was faithful to Abraham, God is faithful to us today.

Another powerful example of God's faithfulness is the story of Joseph. Joseph's life was full of hardships—he was sold into slavery by his brothers, falsely accused, and thrown into prison. But through it all, God was faithful. In the end, Joseph became a powerful leader in Egypt, and God used him to save his family and many others from famine. Even when things seemed hopeless, Joseph trusted in God's faithfulness, and God's plan came to pass.

We all make mistakes. There are times when we think, say, or do things we know are wrong. But one of the most amazing things about God is that He is always ready to forgive. No matter how far we've wandered or how badly we've messed up, God's forgiveness is always available to us. All we have to do is ask.

A great story that shows God's forgiveness is the story of King David. David was a man after God's own heart, but he wasn't perfect. In 2 Samuel 11, we see how David committed adultery with Bathsheba and then tried to cover it up by having her husband killed. It was a terrible sin. But when David was confronted with his wrongdoing, he repented and asked God for forgiveness. Psalm 51 is David's prayer of repentance, and in it, he asks God to create a clean heart within him. Despite David's mistakes, God forgave David and continued to use him in incredible ways. This story shows us that no matter how much we've messed up, God's grace is greater. As 1 John 1:9 (ESV) reminds us, "If we confess our sins, He is faithful and just to forgive us our sins and to cleanse us from all unrighteousness."

Sometimes life doesn't make sense. We go through hard times, and it's easy to wonder, *Why is this happening?* But the Bible teaches us that God has a plan for each of our lives, and His plan is always good, even when we can't see it. Jeremiah 29:11 says, "'For I know the plans I have for you,' declares the LORD, plans to prosper you and not to harm you, plans to give you hope and a future."

One story that shows us how God's plan is commendable is the story of Esther. In the book of Esther, we meet a young Jewish woman who became queen of Persia. When her people were threatened with destruction, Esther risked her life to go before the king and plead for their safety. Because of her courage and obedience to God, the Jewish people were saved. Esther didn't know at first why she was chosen to be queen, but in the end, she realized that God had placed her in that position "for such a time as this" (Esther 4:14). God's plan was at work behind the scenes all along.

When we stop and reflect on everything about God—His unmatched power, His unconditional love, His unwavering faithfulness, His grace-filled forgiveness, and His perfect plan for our lives—it's clear that He is more than worthy of our praise. We might admire people in our lives or look up to others, but no one compares to God. His commendable nature inspires us not only to praise Him but also to live in a way that reflects His goodness to others.

So as we think about what is commendable, let's always start by looking at God. He is the ultimate example of what it means to be worthy of praise, and He invites us to live lives that reflect His goodness.

Do you ever scroll through social media and see someone post about their accomplishments? Maybe they got a promotion at work, ran their first marathon, or won an award. What's your first reaction? If you're anything like me, sometimes that first thought isn't very commendable. Sometimes it's "must be nice" or "they probably had help" or even "they're just showing off." But God calls us to think about whatever is commendable—to celebrate others' victories, to praise good things, to focus on what's worthy of honor.

I remember sitting in church one Sunday when our pastor asked us to think about the last time we genuinely celebrated someone else's success. Not just a quick "congratulations" text, but real, heartfelt joy for another person's achievement. I sat there feeling convicted because I couldn't remember the last time I had done that. Instead, I had been letting comparison steal my joy and prevent me from seeing what was truly commendable in others.

The word *commendable* in Philippians 4:8 comes from the Greek word *euphēmos*, which means "worthy of praise" or "speaking well of." It's about recognizing and celebrating what is good, noble, and praiseworthy. But here's the thing—we live in a world that's quick to criticize and slow to commend. We're more likely to leave a negative review than a positive one. More likely to point out what's wrong than what's right. More likely to tear down than build up.

The Bible is full of examples of commendable behavior and God's recognition of it. Let's dive into some of these stories that show us what truly deserves praise and recognition in God's eyes.

Remember Joseph? Talk about someone who lived a commendable life in difficult circumstances! Sold into slavery by his own brothers, falsely accused by Potiphar's wife, forgotten in prison—yet at every turn, Joseph chose to act with integrity and honor. Even when no one was watching, when he could have sought revenge or given in to bitterness, he remained faithful to God. Genesis 39:4 tells us that he found favor in

Potiphar's eyes because of his commendable behavior. Later, when he had the power to punish his brothers, he chose forgiveness and reconciliation instead. That's commendable!

Or consider Esther, who showed commendable courage when she approached the king uninvited, an act that could have cost her life. But what strikes me most about Esther's story is that before she took that brave step, she spent three days in prayer and fasting. She didn't rush in with her own agenda; she sought God's guidance first. Her words "if I perish, I perish" (Esther 4:16) show a commendable commitment to doing what's right, regardless of the cost.

Jesus himself pointed out commendable behavior in unexpected places. When a Roman centurion— someone who wasn't even part of God's chosen people—showed remarkable faith, Jesus didn't minimize it or ignore it. Instead, He turned to the crowd and said, "Truly I tell you, I have not found anyone in Israel with such great faith" (Matthew 8:10). Jesus commended faith wherever He found it. He praised the widow who gave her last coins, not because of the amount but because of her heart (Mark 12:41–44). He celebrated when people got it right.

One of my favorite examples is Barnabas, whose name actually means "son of encouragement." In Acts 9:27, when everyone else was afraid of Paul (then Saul) and doubted his conversion, Barnabas stood up for him and vouched for the genuineness of his faith. Later, in Acts 15:37–39, Barnabas wanted to give John

Mark (or Mark) a second chance when Paul didn't think it was wise. Time proved Barnabas's commendable spirit of encouragement to be right; Mark later became someone Paul considered valuable to the ministry (2 Timothy 4:11).

Think about the commendable faith of the four friends who lowered their paralyzed friend through a roof to get him to Jesus (Mark 2:1–12). They didn't let obstacles stop them. They didn't worry about property damage or what people would think. They focused on getting their friend to Jesus, and their faith was commended.

I struggled with this concept during my sophomore year of college. There was this girl on my track team who always seemed to get personal bests and first place finishes without much effort. While everyone else was working their butt off in practice, she would show up late sometimes or mention that she didn't do the workouts over break. At first, I found myself making excuses: "She probably cheats," or "The coaches like her more because she's better." But God convicted me about these thoughts. They weren't commendable. They weren't worthy of praise. They were rooted in jealousy and insecurity.

Through prayer and intentional mind-set shifts, I started to see things differently. This girl wasn't my competition; she was my sister in Christ. Her success didn't diminish my worth. When I finally approached her and genuinely asked about her practicing habits, I discovered she had developed an incredibly efficient system that she was happy to share. My resentment had been blocking me from learning from someone who could have been helping me all along.

This reminds me of another powerful biblical example: Jonathan's commendable attitude toward David. As Saul's son, Jonathan had every human reason to view David as competition. David's success could have threatened Jonathan's future kingship. But instead of jealousy, Jonathan showed remarkable friendship and support. He celebrated David's successes and even gave him his own robe and weapons (1 Samuel 18:4)—a powerful symbolic gesture of support. Jonathan's commendable attitude stands in stark contrast to the jealous rage of his father, Saul.

Speaking of David, let's talk about his commendable behavior when he had the chance to kill Saul in a cave (1 Samuel 24). Even though Saul was trying to kill him, even though his men were urging him to take this opportunity, David refused to harm the Lord's anointed. He chose to honor God's timing rather than take matters into his own hands. That's what commendable behavior looks like—choosing God's way even when an easier or more personally beneficial option is available.

But being commendable isn't just about praising others; it's also about living a life worthy of commendation. In 1 Peter 2:12, we're called to live such good lives among unbelievers that they may see our good deeds and glorify God. This doesn't mean performing good deeds for show or seeking praise from others. In fact, 2 Corinthians 10:18 reminds us that "it is not the one who commends himself who is approved, but the one whom the Lord commends."

Think about Daniel in the Bible. He lived a commendable life not by drawing attention to himself but by staying faithful to God even when it could have cost him his life. His commitment to prayer, even when it was forbidden, showed what he valued most. His integrity in his work was so outstanding that even his enemies couldn't find fault with him except concerning his faith (Daniel 6:4–5). That's commendable!

Ruth showed commendable loyalty to Naomi and to God, leaving behind everything familiar to follow Him. Her words "Your people will be my people and your God my God" demonstrate a commendable commitment that went far beyond mere duty (Ruth 1:16). These weren't one-time actions; they were lifestyle choices that consistently honored God.

I've seen this played out in modern life through my good friend Sarah. She's a high school teacher who never seeks the spotlight, but her life consistently points others to Christ. When students are struggling, she stays late to help them. When colleagues are going through hard times, she's the first to organize meals and support. She doesn't post about these things on social media or expect recognition. She simply lives a life that's commendable because she's focused on honoring God.

Let me share another personal story that taught me about commendable behavior. During my freshman year, I was part of a group project where one team member wasn't pulling their weight. The rest of us were frustrated and planning to tell the professor. But one girl in our group took a different approach. Instead of complaining, she reached out to the struggling student and discovered he was dealing with severe anxiety and family issues. Rachel spent extra time helping him catch up and even helped him connect with campus resources. Her commendable response not only saved our project but also showed Christ's love in action.

The challenge for us is to cultivate both aspects of "whatever is commendable": celebrating what is praiseworthy in others and living lives worthy of commendation ourselves. This starts in our thought life. When we catch ourselves thinking critically about others' successes, we need to pause and redirect our thoughts. When we're tempted to do something just for show or recognition, we need to check our motivations.

Sometimes living a commendable life means making unpopular choices. I experienced this during my junior year when I chose not to participate in a team activity that involved drinking games. Several teammates were angry with me, saying I was ruining team bonding. But I knew that their drinking, even if considered "mild," wasn't commendable behavior. Standing firm in that decision was hard, but it actually led to conversations about why certain team activities needed to change.

This reminds me of Shadrach, Meshach, and Abednego. Talk about making an unpopular choice!

When everyone else was bowing to the golden image, they stood firm in their faith. Their response to the king in Daniel 3:17–18 (ESV) is one of the most commendable statements in Scripture: "Our God whom we serve is able to deliver us . . . But if not, be it known to you, O king, that we will not serve your gods." They were commendable not just in their refusal to bow but in their trust in God regardless of the outcome.

Here's what I've learned about thinking on whatever is commendable.

First, it requires intentionality. Our natural tendency isn't always to celebrate others or to make choices that honor God. We have to deliberately direct our thoughts toward what is praiseworthy. Like Paul says in 2 Corinthians 10:5 (ESV), we need to "take every thought captive to obey Christ."

Second, it involves humility. Recognizing what is commendable in others means setting aside our own pride and competitive nature. Living a commendable life means doing what's right even when no one is watching or applauding. Remember John the Baptist's commendable humility when he said of Jesus, "He must increase, but I must decrease" (John 3:30 ESV).

Third, it's connected to gratitude. When we're thankful for what God has done in our lives, it's easier to celebrate what He's doing in others' lives. Gratitude helps us see the commendable things we might otherwise miss. Think of the leper who returned to thank Jesus; Jesus specifically commended his grateful heart (Luke 17:11–19).

Fourth, it's about perspective. What the world considers commendable isn't always what God considers commendable. We need to align our values with His Word to recognize true worth. Remember how Jesus commended Mary's choice to sit at His feet while Martha was busy with preparations (Luke 10:38–42)? Sometimes the most commendable thing is simply choosing to focus on Jesus.

I learned this lesson in a powerful way during my high school years. I was up for a prestigious leadership position in FBLA (Future Business Leaders of America), and I had worked incredibly hard to build my résumé. When I didn't get it, I was devastated. But through that disappointment, God showed me how much of my effort had been focused on appearing commendable to others rather than truly living a life worthy of His commendation. It was a humbling but necessary lesson.

The beautiful thing about focusing on whatever is commendable is that it changes us from the inside out. When we train our minds to look for what is praiseworthy, we start to see more of it. When we commit to living lives worthy of commendation, we find ourselves making different choices. And ultimately, this mind-set shift brings glory to God, who is the source of everything truly commendable.

Let me share one final biblical example that always challenges me. In Acts 16, Paul and Silas are singing hymns and praising God while in prison. That's commendable! They weren't just enduring their circumstances; they were choosing to praise God in them. Their commendable behavior not only led to their own deliverance but also to the salvation of the jailer and his family. That's what can happen when we choose to think about and live out whatever is commendable—it impacts not just us but everyone around us.

So the next time you scroll through social media and see someone's success, pause and ask yourself: *How can I genuinely celebrate this person?* When faced with a choice between what's popular and what's right, remember that God commends faithfulness over fame. In every situation, look for what is worthy of praise—not to gain approval from others but to honor the God who has called us to think about whatever is commendable.

Remember, commendable thinking isn't about perfection; it's about direction. It's about consistently choosing to focus our thoughts on what is worthy of praise and striving to live in a way that brings glory to God. As we fix our minds on whatever is commendable, we'll find ourselves being transformed more and more into the image of Christ, who is ultimately the most commendable example we could ever follow.

PRACTICE

Now that we've explored what it means to be commendable, let's make it personal. God calls us not just to admire what's praiseworthy but to live it out. Here are some activities and reflections to help you do just that.

1. Reflection: Whom Do You Admire?

Think of someone you admire—maybe a family member or a friend. What makes them commendable in your eyes? Write down their qualities and reflect on how they live in a way that's worthy of respect.

   - What qualities make them praiseworthy?
   - How can you reflect those same qualities in your life?

2. Bible Study: Commendable Lives in Scripture

Read about these biblical figures:

   - Joseph (Genesis 37–50)—His faithfulness through hardship is commendable.
   - Esther (Esther 4:14)—Her bravery in saving her people reflects courage.
   - Ruth (Ruth 1:16–18)—Her loyalty shows faithfulness.

Reflect on these questions:

   - What commendable qualities do you see in these stories?
   - How can you apply them in your life?

3. Praise Journal: Praise the Lord Through Journaling

For one week, keep a journal where you write down something praiseworthy about God each day. This could be something you see in His creation, an answered prayer, or a verse that reminds you of His faithfulness.

At the end of the week, reflect on how this practice has deepened your appreciation for God's commendable nature.

4. Self-Check: Living a Commendable Life

Take a moment to reflect on your own life:

- What actions of yours reflect something commendable?
- What areas need growth?

Choose one specific area to work on this week, such as speaking kindly to others or acting with integrity.

5. Prayer Reflection: Ask God to Help You

End this section with a prayer, asking God to help you live a commendable life. Ask Him for strength, wisdom, and opportunities to reflect His goodness.

Whatever Is

JOURNAL

7

Excellent

THINK

"I just need to get through this day."

How many times have you whispered these words to yourself? Maybe it was while trying to manage a busy household, during a stressful work presentation, or in the middle of a challenging season of life. I know I've said them more times than I can count. But here's what God showed me: He didn't create us just to "get through" our days. He created us for excellence.

Now, before you close this book thinking, *I can't handle one more thing I need to excel at*, let me share something that changed my perspective entirely. This isn't about adding another item to your already overwhelming to-do list. It's not about being the perfect mom, the ideal wife, the star employee, or the most dedicated church volunteer. It's about transforming how we think about excellence itself.

I remember the day this hit me hard. I was in Target's home organization aisle (because where else do we go when we need to feel like we're getting our life together?), looking at planners and containers, convinced that if I just found the right system, I could finally excel at, well, everything. My cart was full of items promising to help me be more organized, more productive, more excellent. Then my phone buzzed with a text from a friend: "Can we talk? I'm really struggling."

In that moment, God spoke to my heart. While I was focused on external excellence—trying to organize my way to a better life—true excellence was calling in the form of a friend who needed support. I left my cart right there in the aisle (sorry, Target employees!) and went to meet my friend for coffee.

That coffee meeting changed both of us. As my friend poured out her heart about her struggling relationships and feelings of inadequacy, I realized that true excellence was happening right there in that messy, tear-filled conversation. No perfectly organized pantry could compare to the sacred space of two hearts connecting in authentic vulnerability.

The word *excellent* in Philippians 4:8 comes from the Greek word *arete*, meaning moral excellence and virtue. But what does that look like for us as women today? It's not about having the most organized pantry (though there's nothing wrong with that), the most perfectly behaved children, or the most impressive career. It's about cultivating excellence in our hearts and minds first.

When we dig deeper into Scripture, we find that God's view of excellence often contradicts our cultural understanding. Think about Jesus's ministry; He consistently chose relationships over rigid rules, mercy over meticulous observance, and heart transformation over external perfection. He found excellence in the widow's mite, the shepherd leaving the ninety-nine to find one lost sheep, and the Samaritan woman's honest confession at the well.

Let's look at some women in the Bible who exemplified true excellence. Take Abigail—now, there's a woman who understood excellence in crisis management! When her foolish husband insulted David and put their entire household in danger, she quickly gathered provisions and intercepted David's army. But it wasn't just her quick thinking that made her excellent; it was her ability to speak truth with grace and wisdom (1 Samuel 25). She didn't just solve a problem; she transformed a potential bloodbath into a moment of blessing.

Consider how different Abigail's excellence looked from what we might expect. She didn't have time to present a perfect appearance or prepare an elaborate speech. Her excellence shone through in her wisdom, courage, and ability to act decisively in alignment with God's purposes. How often do we miss opportunities for true excellence because we're too focused on perfecting the superficial?

Or consider Priscilla, who along with her husband, Aquila, demonstrated excellence in discipleship. They didn't just offer surface-level hospitality; they took Apollo aside and "explained to him the way of God more adequately" (Acts 18:26). Their excellence wasn't about having a perfect home for hosting; it was about excellence in building God's kingdom through intentional relationships.

What strikes me about Priscilla is that she didn't wait until she had achieved some arbitrary standard of theological expertise before investing in others. She and Aquila simply shared what they knew with humility and authenticity. This challenges our tendency to wait until we feel "excellent enough" before stepping into ministry opportunities.

I used to struggle with feeling like I was never excellent enough. My apartment wasn't as clean as my neighbor's, my designing style wasn't as cute as my cousins, and my quiet time with God wasn't as consistent as my small group leader's. But then I read about Mary and Martha, and something clicked. When Martha was distracted by all the preparations that had to be made, Jesus told her that Mary had chosen what was better—sitting at His feet and learning from Him.

This story particularly resonates with me because I am, by nature, such a Martha. I want to do everything right, to serve perfectly, to make sure all the details are handled with excellence. But Jesus gently redirects our understanding of excellence. He shows us that sometimes excellence means choosing presence over performance, relationship over routine, and learning over doing.

This doesn't mean we shouldn't strive for excellence in our daily tasks. Rather, it means we need to redefine what excellence looks like through God's eyes. Sometimes excellence is choosing to sit and listen when there's laundry to be folded. Sometimes it's letting your kids make a mess while baking cookies because relationship building is more excellent than a spotless kitchen.

I've learned this lesson the hard way, particularly in my role as a babysitter. I remember one afternoon when I was trying to help this little girl with her homework while simultaneously preparing dinner, answering school emails, and mentally planning tomorrow's schedule. I was aiming for excellence in productivity, but I was missing excellence in presence. When I saw the frustration in the little girl's eyes, I knew something had to change.

Let me share a personal story that taught me about true excellence. I was leading a women's Bible study, and I was so focused on having the perfect points and clever object lessons that I almost missed the real excellence happening in our group. It was in the way one woman vulnerably shared her struggle with infertility and another immediately offered to pray with her after the study. It was in the young mom who hadn't had time to do the homework but came anyway because she desperately needed community. Excellence was happening in these authentic connections, not in my perfectly prepared presentation.

That experience revolutionized how I lead Bible studies. Instead of obsessing over perfect presentations, I focus on creating space for authentic sharing and genuine community. I've learned that excellence in ministry often looks more like being present and responsive to the Holy Spirit's leading than executing a flawless plan.

The Bible shows us that excellence often looks different than we expect. Look at Ruth—her excellence wasn't in doing extraordinary things but in being faithful in ordinary things. She didn't just gather leftover grain; she did it with such excellence that Boaz noticed her character before her circumstances.

Ruth's story particularly challenges our modern notion of excellence. In a world that celebrates viral moments and overnight success stories, Ruth's excellence was displayed in daily faithfulness, loyal love, and humble service. She wasn't seeking recognition or trying to prove herself; she was simply living out her commitment to God and Naomi with excellence of character.

Sometimes we hesitate to pursue excellence because we're afraid of appearing prideful. But think about Lydia in Acts 16:11–15. She was a successful businesswoman who dealt in purple cloth, a luxury item. Her excellence in business didn't diminish her excellence in faith; instead, she used her success to bless others by hosting Paul and his companions.

Lydia's example teaches us that excellence in our professional lives can coexist beautifully with excellence in our spiritual lives. She didn't compartmentalize her faith but allowed it to influence every aspect of her life. Her excellence in business became a platform for ministry and kingdom impact.

Here's what I've learned about thinking on whatever is excellent.

First, excellence starts with our thought life. It's about training our minds to focus on what truly matters. When I catch myself scrolling through Instagram comparing my messy mom bun to someone else's perfectly styled hair, I have to actively redirect my thoughts to what God considers excellent.

This mental retraining isn't easy. It requires constant vigilance and regular reality checks. I've started asking myself, *Will this matter in eternity?* When I'm tempted to berate myself for not measuring up to some arbitrary standard of excellence, this question helps me refocus on what truly matters.

Second, excellence is about stewardship, not perfectionism. Remember the parable of the talents? The servants who were commended weren't perfect; they were faithful with what they had been given. Excellence means faithfully using whatever God has given us— whether that's being present with our toddler during the thousandth reading of their favorite book or using our professional skills to serve in our church.

I've found this principle particularly freeing when it comes to using my gifts in ministry. I used to hold back from serving because I didn't feel excellent enough compared to others. But when I started viewing excellence through the lens of stewardship, it changed everything. The question became not "Am I the best at this?" but "Am I being faithful with what God has given me?"

Third, excellence is contagious. When we pursue true excellence—the kind that flows from a heart aligned with God—it inspires others. I've seen this in my own life when younger women have told me they were encouraged by seeing me be real about my struggles while still pursuing God's best.

This kind of excellence creates a ripple effect in our communities. When we're authentic about our journey toward excellence, including our failures and struggles, it gives others permission to be real too. It creates an environment where true growth can happen.

Fourth, excellence requires rest. This might seem counterintuitive, but even God rested after creation. Excellence doesn't mean running ourselves ragged; it means honoring God's rhythms of work and rest.

I've had to learn this lesson repeatedly. As someone who naturally tends toward overachievement, accepting rest as part of excellence has been challenging. But I've discovered that some of my most excellent moments come after times of intentional rest, when I'm operating from a place of fullness rather than depletion.

Let me share another story that reshaped my understanding of excellence. I was feeling guilty about missing my morning quiet time because I had a late night at youth group the night before. In the morning, as I sat at a table across from one of my youth group girls, God reminded me that excellence in that moment looked like loving His child with patience and grace. Sometimes excellence is found in these small, unseen moments of faithfulness.

That morning taught me something profound about excellence in youth ministry. It's not about maintaining a perfect schedule or never missing a devotional time. It's about being present in each moment, responding to youth group members' needs with love, and modeling what it looks like to depend on God's grace.

The pursuit of excellence in our thought life transforms every aspect of our lives. When we think about whatever is excellent, we

- stop comparing our behind-the-scenes with everyone else's highlight reel
- find contentment in doing our best for God's glory rather than others' approval
- recognize excellence in ordinary moments, not just big achievements
- extend grace to ourselves and others while still pursuing growth
- focus on internal transformation rather than external perfection

This transformation doesn't happen overnight. It's a journey of daily choices and constant course corrections. I'm still learning to catch myself when I start slipping back into worldly definitions of excellence.

I've found that excellence often shows up most powerfully in how we handle life's interruptions. Like the woman with the issue of blood who pursued Jesus for healing—her excellent faith led her to reach out despite cultural barriers and physical weakness. Or like Dorcas, whose excellence was demonstrated in the consistent kindness of making clothes for widows.

These biblical examples challenge our tendency to view interruptions as obstacles to excellence. Instead, they show us that excellence often emerges in how we respond to the unexpected, the inconvenient, and the challenging moments of life.

Let me share some practical ways I've learned to cultivate excellent thinking.

Start your day by asking, *God, what does excellence look like for today?* Sometimes His answer might surprise you. Last week, excellence looked like canceling my carefully planned schedule to sit with a grieving friend.

Keep a "divine excellence" journal where you record moments when you see God's definition of excellence play out—in Scripture, in your life, in others. This practice helps retrain our minds to recognize true excellence.

Practice excellent self-talk by speaking truth over yourself. Instead of *I'm such a mess*, try *I'm growing in excellence as I learn to depend on God.* Our internal dialogue shapes our understanding of excellence.

Create an "excellence filter" for your thoughts: Does this thought align with God's excellence? Does it build up or tear down? This simple tool has helped me catch and redirect thoughts that don't align with God's definition of excellence.

I've also found it helpful to create "excellence anchors"—specific Scripture verses or truths that remind me of what true excellence looks like. When I feel myself getting caught up in perfectionism or comparison, I return to these anchors to reset my perspective.

The beautiful thing about focusing on whatever is excellent is that it frees us from the world's exhausting standards of excellence. We don't have to excel at everything; we just need to excel at being who God created us to be.

This truth has been particularly liberating in my relationships. Instead of trying to be the perfect friend who never says the wrong thing and always knows exactly how to help, I can focus on being authentically present and consistently loving. Excellence in relationships isn't about perfection; it's about genuine connection and growth.

Remember that excellent woman described in Proverbs 31? Notice that the passage doesn't say she did everything perfectly. Instead, it describes a woman who faced each task and relationship with excellence of character. She wasn't afraid of the future because her excellence came from her fear of the Lord, not her own capabilities.

What strikes me most about the Proverbs 31 woman is that her excellence was multifaceted. She wasn't excellent in just one area of life; she brought excellence to everything she did, not through superhuman perfection but through wisdom, diligence, and fear of the Lord.

So the next time you're tempted to believe you're not excellent enough—whether as a mom, wife, friend, professional, or follower of Christ—remember this: Excellence isn't about reaching some impossible standard. It's about training our minds to focus on what God says is excellent and letting that transform how we live.

This journey toward biblical excellence is ongoing. Just yesterday, I caught myself slipping back into performance-based thinking. I was preparing to speak in front of the church congregation on Sunday, and I found myself obsessing over having the perfect outfit, the most engaging introduction, the most memorable illustrations. God gently reminded me that true excellence wasn't in the perfection of my presentation but in the authenticity of my message and my willingness to be used by Him.

True excellence isn't found in perfect performance but in a heart perfectly aligned with God's purposes. When we fix our thoughts on whatever is excellent, we begin to see ourselves and our daily lives through His eyes—and that changes everything.

The transformation happens gradually, like a garden growing. Some days, you might not see much progress. Other days, you notice new growth sprouting up where there used to be only bare soil. The key is to keep tending the garden of excellence in our thoughts, pulling out the weeds of comparison and perfectionism, and nurturing the seeds of truth that God has planted.

Isn't it beautiful that God doesn't call us to be excellent at everything, but rather to think about whatever is excellent? As we do, He transforms our minds, and through that transformation, we become more like Him—the author and perfecter of our faith, the truly excellent One.

Remember, dear sister, that your journey toward excellence is unique. God's definition of excellence for your life might look very different from what it looks like for someone else's life. Embrace that uniqueness. Trust that as you fix your thoughts on what is excellent, God will continue to shape and mold you into His image, one thought at a time.

PRACTICE

Set aside two to three hours for this practice. Find a quiet space where you won't be interrupted. You'll need the following:

- A mirror
- Paper and pen
- Your Bible
- A blank sheet of paper
- Colored markers or pencils

Part 1: The Mirror Moment Sit

Stand or sit in front of your mirror. Look at yourself for a full minute (set a timer). Then write down

- what you see
- what you wish you saw
- what you think God sees

Part 2: The Excellence Tree

On a piece of paper, draw a large tree on your paper. Then complete the following steps:

- In the roots, write the sources of your current definition of excellence (parents, teachers, society, church, friends, etc.).
- On the trunk, write your current struggles with excellence.
- On the branches, write God's truths about excellence from Scripture.
- On the leaves, write new ways you want to view excellence.

Part 3: The Three Chairs

Set up three chairs (or spaces) with the following labels:

- Chair 1: "World's Excellence"
- Chair 2: "My Excellence"
- Chair 3: "God's Excellence"

Sit in each chair for five minutes. Chair 1: Write down the demands and expectations you feel from the world. Chair 2: Write down your personal standards and pressures you put on yourself. Chair 3: Write down what you hear God saying about excellence

Part 4: The Release

Take all your notes from Chair 1 and Chair 2. Read them one last time, then go through the following steps:

- Cross out anything that contradicts God's truth.
- Circle anything that aligns with God's excellence.
- Create one new definition of excellence based on what you've learned.
- Physically crumple up the paper with the world's demands and throw it away.

Part 5: The Excellence Declaration

- Using everything you've discovered, write
- Three truths about God's excellence
- Three lies about excellence you're letting go

- Three ways you'll pursue true excellence this week
- One prayer for your journey toward God's excellence

Close by reading Philippians 4:8 aloud, emphasizing the word *excellent*.

Excellent

JOURNAL

8

Praiseworthy

THINK

Have you ever noticed how a genuine word of praise can lift your spirit? That moment when someone recognizes something truly worthy in you or your actions? As women, we often deflect praise, brushing it aside with "Oh, it was nothing" or quickly redirecting attention to someone else. Yet God's Word tells us explicitly to dwell on things that are praiseworthy—not just to give praise but to meditate on what deserves praise.

In the original Greek, the word used for *praiseworthy* in Philippians 4:8 is *epainos*, which refers to something worthy of praise, commendation, or approval. It's not about empty flattery or seeking attention, but rather recognizing and dwelling on what truly deserves honor before God.

This distinction is crucial in our social media age, where praise often feels like currency. We double-tap photos, leave quick compliments, and share encouraging emojis—but are we truly dwelling on what is praiseworthy? Are we training our minds to recognize and meditate on things that deserve genuine honor before God?

Let me tell you about something that happened to me last month. I was struggling with my prayer life, feeling like my words were hollow and repetitive. One morning, while reading my Bible, I came across Psalm 145, where David spends the entire chapter just praising God's attributes. It hit me: I had been approaching prayer all wrong. Instead of focusing on what I needed or wanted, I needed to focus my thoughts on what was truly praiseworthy about God's character.

That morning changed my entire approach to prayer. Instead of launching into my requests, I began starting each prayer time by listing God's attributes. His faithfulness. His wisdom. His mercy. His justice. His love. It wasn't just about saying the words; it was about truly meditating on each characteristic, letting my mind dwell on concrete examples of how I'd seen these attributes displayed in my life and in Scripture.

You know what's amazing about praise? It's not just something we do; it's something that transforms us. When David was running from Saul, hiding in caves, what did he write? Psalms of praise! In Psalm 34:1, he declares, "I will extol the LORD at all times; his praise will always be on my lips." Notice he didn't say "when things are good" or "when I feel like it." He chose to focus on what was praiseworthy even in the darkest times.

This reminds me of a powerful lesson I learned from a lady I thought of as my grandmother. During the last years of her life, she battled severe arthritis that left her largely homebound. Yet every time I visited her, she had a new praise report. One day I asked her how she managed to stay so positive. Her response changed my perspective forever. "Honey," she said, "when your body won't let you do much, your mind becomes your garden. I've chosen to plant praise there."

I learned this lesson in a powerful way during my time in college track. I had been dealing with some health issues that were affecting my running. Every day was a struggle, and I found myself constantly complaining about what I couldn't do. Then one day a mentor pulled me aside and said something I'll never forget: "Instead of focusing on what your body can't do, why don't you praise God for what it can do?" That shifted everything for me. I started praising God for the ability to walk, to breathe, to move at all. My circumstances hadn't changed, but my focus had.

The transformation wasn't instant. I had to deliberately retrain my thoughts, catching myself whenever I started spiraling into complaints or self-pity. I started keeping what I called a "praise portfolio"—a simple notebook where I documented daily evidence of God's goodness, no matter how small. Some days, my entries were as basic as "I can take deep breaths without pain." Other days, they were filled with bigger victories. But each entry helped reshape my thought patterns.

Let's talk about Jehoshaphat for a minute. In 2 Chronicles 20, when three armies were coming against Judah, what did he do? He put the praise singers at the front of the army! Can you imagine? The situation looked hopeless, but he chose to focus on what was praiseworthy: God's faithfulness, His power, His promises. And God came through in an amazing way.

What strikes me most about this story is the timing. Jehoshaphat didn't wait until after the victory to arrange the praise singers. He put them at the front of the army before the battle even began. That's radical praise—choosing to focus on God's praiseworthy character before seeing the solution to problems.

This reminds me of my friend Neenah. She lost her mom to cancer last year, and in the midst of her grief, she started what she calls her "praise journal." Every day, she writes down one praiseworthy attribute of God she sees in her life. Some days it's big things, like provision for medical bills. Other days it's small things, like the warmth of sunshine. But she's training her mind to look for what's praiseworthy, even in her pain.

Neenah's journey taught me something profound about praise: It's not about denying our pain or pretending everything is fine. It's about choosing to acknowledge God's praiseworthy character even in the midst of our struggles. Some days, her journal entries are tear stained. Some days, they're just a single word. But each entry is an act of choosing to focus on what is praiseworthy, even when praise feels like a sacrifice.

You know what else is praiseworthy? The fact that God uses broken people for His glory. Think about Moses—a murderer turned deliverer. Or Peter—the disciple who denied Jesus three times but became a pillar of the early church. When we focus our thoughts on how God transforms lives, it gives us hope for our own journey.

I see this truth playing out in my own community. There's a woman in my church who struggled with addiction for twenty years. Today she is a leader in our church's prayer ministry. When she shares her testimony, she never glorifies her past, but she praises God for His redemptive power. Her life is a walking testament to what is truly praiseworthy—not our own strength or abilities but God's transformative grace.

Sometimes I find myself getting caught up in the world's definition of what's praiseworthy. Success, achievement, popularity—these things aren't bad in themselves, but they're not the highest good. I remember sitting in a church one night at a leader's conference listening to a missionary share about her work in a remote village. No one knew her name. She didn't have a big social media following. But as she shared about God's faithfulness in bringing just one person to Christ, her face lit up with genuine praise. That's when I realized I had been measuring praise by the wrong standards.

This realization led me to examine my own "praise triggers." What automatically prompts me to offer praise? A high grade? A compliment on my appearance? A successful event? While none of these things are wrong, I began asking God to help me develop new praise triggers. The evidence of His work in someone's life. The beauty of His creation. The truth of His Word. The fellowship of His people.

The Bible shows us example after example of what God considers praiseworthy. Look at the widow who gave her last two coins (Mark 12:41–44). Jesus praised her not because of how much she gave but because of her heart. Or consider Mary of Bethany, who was praised by Jesus for choosing to sit at His feet while everyone else was busy with other things (Luke 10:38–42). What's praiseworthy to God often looks very different from what the world praises.

This contrast becomes even clearer when we look at the Beatitudes. Jesus pronounces blessings—a form of praise—on those who are poor in spirit, those who mourn, those who are meek, and those who hunger and thirst for righteousness. These aren't typically the qualities that get praise on social media or in performance reviews, but they're precisely what God considers worthy of blessing.

I've noticed something interesting in my own life: when I focus on praising God for who He is, my anxiety levels drop. It's like what Paul says in Philippians 4:6: "Do not be anxious about anything, but in every situation, by prayer and petition, with thanksgiving, present your requests to God." Did you catch that? Thanksgiving, or praise, comes before peace.

This connection between praise and peace isn't just spiritual theory; it's backed by research showing that gratitude and praise actually affect our brain chemistry. But more importantly, it's a spiritual principle that God wove into the fabric of our being. We were created to praise, and when we align our thoughts with what is truly praiseworthy, we find ourselves operating the way we were designed to function.

Recently, I was stressing about a sermon I was going to give—my first one! The night before, instead of rehearsing my sermon for the hundredth time, I decided to spend time praising God for His attributes. I praised Him for His wisdom, His sovereignty, His care for every detail of my life. Something amazing happened: my focus shifted from my performance to His faithfulness. I still gave the sermon, but my mind was anchored in something more praiseworthy than my own abilities.

That experience taught me something crucial about praise: it's not just about the words we say; it's about where we choose to fix our attention. When we truly focus on what is praiseworthy about God's character, everything else naturally falls into proper perspective. Our challenges don't disappear, but they no longer dominate our thinking.

You know who really understood praise? The early church. In Acts we see believers praising God when they were persecuted (Acts 5:41), when they were imprisoned (Acts 16:25), even when they faced death (Acts 7:59–60). They understood something we often forget, that God's worthiness of praise doesn't depend on our circumstances.

Their example challenges me deeply. How often do I let circumstances dictate my praise? How frequently do I allow temporary setbacks to overshadow eternal truths? The early church reminds us that true praise isn't reactive to circumstances; it's rooted in the unchanging character of God.

Think about Paul and Silas in that Philippian jail. They had been beaten, thrown in prison, their feet locked in stocks. And what were they doing at midnight? Singing hymns of praise! They weren't praising God because things were good; they were praising God because He is good. Their situation hadn't changed, but their focus was on something praiseworthy beyond their circumstances.

This story has practical implications for our daily lives. When we face our own "prison moments"— whether it's a difficult relationship, a health challenge, a financial struggle, or any other trial—we have a choice. We can focus on the chains that bind us, or we can focus on the God who is worthy of praise regardless of our circumstances.

I want to challenge you with something I've been learning. Every time you open social media, every time you face a difficult situation, every time you're tempted to compare yourself to others, pause and ask yourself: *What's praiseworthy here?* Not in a superficial way but really looking for evidence of God's character and work.

This practice has transformed how I use social media. Instead of getting caught in the comparison trap, I've started looking for evidence of God's praiseworthy work in others' lives. A friend's new job becomes an opportunity to praise God's provision. A wedding announcement becomes a chance to praise His design for relationships. Even difficult posts about struggles become opportunities to praise His faithfulness in the midst of trials.

The prophet Habakkuk shows us what this looks like. At the end of his book, even though everything was going wrong—no flowers, no fruit, no food, no flocks—he declares, "Yet I will rejoice in the LORD, I will be joyful in God my Savior" (Habakkuk 3:17–18). He chose to focus on what was eternally praiseworthy rather than temporary circumstances.

Habakkuk's declaration isn't just poetic; it's practical. He lists all the things going wrong—a complete agricultural and economic disaster in his context—but then makes a deliberate choice to focus on what remains praiseworthy. This isn't denial; it's perspective. He acknowledges the reality of his circumstances while choosing to fix his thoughts on something more worthy of his attention.

Sometimes praise feels like a sacrifice. Hebrews 13:15 talks about offering a "sacrifice of praise"—that means praising even when we don't feel like it. But here's what I've discovered: the more we practice looking for what's praiseworthy, the more naturally we begin to see it. It's like training your eyes to spot certain birds or flowers: once you know what to look for, you start seeing it everywhere.

This principle of practiced praise has become especially meaningful in my role as a small group leader.

Every week, I challenge my teens to share one praise-worthy thing they've noticed about God's character or work in their lives. At first many of them struggled to come up with examples. But as weeks passed, something beautiful happened: they started coming to the group eager to share what they'd noticed. Their praise muscles were getting stronger through regular exercise.

God's character is always praiseworthy. His faithfulness never fails. His love never ends. His mercy is new every morning. His grace is always sufficient. When we fix our thoughts on these truths, everything else falls into perspective. The challenges don't disappear, but they no longer dominate our thinking.

I've started keeping what I call a "praise repository"—a collection of Bible verses that highlight God's praiseworthy attributes. When I'm struggling to find something praiseworthy in my circumstances, I turn to these verses. They remind me that praise isn't dependent on my situation; it's anchored in God's unchanging character.

Let me share one final personal story. A few weeks ago, I was having what felt like the worst day ever. Everything that could go wrong did. I was tired, frustrated, and honestly, the last thing I felt like doing was praising God. But I remembered what my Bible study leader had taught me about choosing praise. So I started small. I praised God for the fact that I was breathing. Then for the ability to walk to the gym and work out. Then for the friends who texted to check on me. As I deliberately focused on what was praise-worthy, my perspective started to shift. The circumstances hadn't changed, but my mind was fixed on something greater.

This practice of "praise progression"—starting with small, obvious things and building to deeper truths—has become a valuable tool in my spiritual journey. When praise feels impossible, I start with the basics. I praise God for air in my lungs, for the ability to think and reason, for His Word that guides me. From there I can usually build to praising Him for bigger things—His sovereignty, His wisdom, His perfect timing.

That's the power of thinking about whatever is praiseworthy. It's not about denying reality or pretending everything is perfect. It's about choosing to focus our thoughts on the One who is always worthy of praise, regardless of our circumstances. When we do this, we find ourselves being transformed from the inside out.

This transformation affects every area of our lives. When we train ourselves to look for what is praise-worthy, we become more encouraging to others. We're quicker to notice and affirm God's work in people's lives. We become better at discerning what truly deserves praise versus what the world tells us is praiseworthy.

God is worthy of praise not because of what He does but because of who He is. He is good (Psalm 136:1). He is faithful (Deuteronomy 7:9). He is just (Psalm 25:8). He is merciful (Exodus 34:6). He is love (1 John 4:8).

These truths don't change with our circumstances or feelings. They are always praiseworthy.

And here's something beautiful I've discovered: when we praise God for who He is, we begin to see more clearly who we are in Him. Our identity becomes more securely anchored in His unchanging character rather than our changing circumstances. We find ourselves less dependent on the praise of others because our minds are fixed on what is truly praiseworthy.

And you know what? When we focus our thoughts on these unchanging truths, when we train our minds to look for what is truly praiseworthy, we find ourselves living with a different perspective. Life's challenges remain real, but worship shifts our perspective dramatically. Rather than allowing our difficulties to monopolize our mental landscape, praise redirects our focus heavenward. Like a ship finding safe harbor in a storm, our spirits find anchor not in changing circumstances but in the immovable majesty of our Creator. When we exalt God's worthiness, our problems don't vanish, but they do find their proper place—subordinate to the magnificent reality of who God is. Our hearts, once preoccupied with earthly concerns, now beat to the rhythm of eternity.

This journey of learning to think on what is praiseworthy is ongoing. Every day presents new opportunities to choose our focus. Will we dwell on our problems, or will we fix our thoughts on what is truly worthy of praise? The choice is ours, and that choice shapes not just our day but our entire perspective on life.

Remember, dear friend, that praise isn't just about words; it's about where we choose to fix our attention. When we deliberately focus our thoughts on what is truly praiseworthy, we find ourselves being transformed into people who naturally notice and celebrate God's goodness in every circumstance. And isn't that a praiseworthy transformation in itself?

PRACTICE

Praise Through the Senses—Find a quiet place where you won't be interrupted. You'll need your Bible and thirty minutes.

See: Look around you. Name five things you can see that reveal God's praiseworthy nature. Write how each one reflects His character.

Hear: Close your eyes. List four sounds you can hear. How does each sound remind you of God's praiseworthy attributes?

Touch: Feel different textures around you. Name three different sensations. How does each one remind you of God's care?

Smell: Identify two scents in your environment. How do they remind you of God's presence?

Taste: If possible, take a small sip of water or bite of food. How does this one taste remind you of God's provision?

Conclude by reading Psalm 34 aloud, letting your newly awakened senses absorb the praise within it.

JOURNAL

Conclusion

As we conclude our journey through these transformative words from Philippians 4:8, we find ourselves standing in a garden of possibility. Each word—*true, honorable, just, pure, lovely, commendable, excellent,* and *praiseworthy*—represents not just a concept to understand but a seed to be planted in the soil of our daily thoughts.

Throughout these pages, we've explored how these divine qualities manifested in biblical narratives, from the unwavering truth of God's promises to the pure heart of David, from the honorable conduct of Daniel to the praiseworthy faith of Mary. We've witnessed how these qualities have shaped not only the stories of biblical figures but also the modern-day testimonies shared within these chapters. Consider how Joseph demonstrated what is true and just when he refused to bear false witness against his master's wife, even though it cost him his freedom. Remember how Ruth showed what is honorable and praiseworthy in her steadfast loyalty to Naomi. Reflect on how Esther embodied what is excellent and commendable when she stood up for her people at the risk of her own life. Each word has revealed itself as a facet of God's character, a standard He calls us to embrace, and a filter through which we can process our thoughts.

But knowledge without application remains merely information. That's why each concept was paired with practical exercises—opportunities to cultivate these qualities in your own thought life. These weren't just activities to complete while reading; they were invitations to develop new habits of mind, to rewire your thought patterns according to God's design. You've practiced identifying truth in a world full of deception, cultivating honor in your relationships, pursuing justice in your sphere of influence, protecting purity in your heart and actions, seeking out lovely things in God's creation, encouraging commendable behavior in others, striving for excellence in your work, and celebrating praiseworthy attributes in those around you.

As you close this book, remember that Philippians 4:8 isn't just a list of virtuous concepts; it's a daily invitation to transformation. Every morning brings new opportunities to choose what we will dwell on. Will we let our minds drift toward whatever catches our attention, or will we intentionally direct our thoughts toward what is true, honorable, just, pure, lovely, commendable, excellent, and praiseworthy?

Consider the profound impact these choices can have. When we choose to dwell on what is true, we become more discerning in a world of misinformation. When we focus on what is honorable, our relationships deepen and our character strengthens. When we contemplate what is just, we become advocates for God's righteousness in our communities. When we cherish what is pure, our hearts grow more sensitive to God's holiness. When we seek out what is lovely, we become more attuned to God's beauty in both creation and redemption. When we celebrate what is commendable, we become better encouragers and builders of others. When we pursue what is excellent, we glorify God through our best efforts. When we praise what is praiseworthy, we align our hearts with heaven's values.

The practice chapters have given you tools, but the real work begins now. In a world that bombards us with messages that often contradict these divine qualities, we must make a conscious choice to filter our thoughts through this biblical lens. It might mean changing what we watch, read, or listen to. It might require us to challenge long-held thought patterns or to deliberately redirect our mind when it wanders into territory that doesn't align with these principles.

It could involve starting your day with a prayer of dedication: *Lord, help me to see what is true in today's conversations. Show me what is honorable in my workplace. Guide me toward what is just in my decisions. Protect what is pure in my relationships. Open my eyes to what is lovely in my circumstances. Lead me to encourage what is commendable in others. Strengthen me to pursue what is excellent in my work. Teach me to celebrate what is praiseworthy in my community.*

Remember, this isn't about achieving perfection in our thought life; it's about progress. It's about partnering with the Holy Spirit in the ongoing work of renewal. Each time you choose to direct your thoughts toward one of these qualities, you're participating in your own transformation. Each deliberate thought becomes a brick in the foundation of a renewed mind. Think of it as spiritual muscle memory—the more we practice thinking about these things, the more naturally our minds will gravitate toward them.

The apostle Paul didn't just give us a list of words to memorize; he gave us a pathway to peace. Notice that these instructions come just before his famous words about the peace of God that surpasses all understanding (Philippians 4:7). There's a direct connection between what we choose to think about and the peace we experience in our lives.

When our minds are anchored in truth, we're less likely to be tossed about by lies. When we focus on what is honorable, we're less distracted by scandal and shame. When we dwell on what is just, we find purpose in pursuing God's righteousness. When we cherish what is pure, we're less troubled by corruption. When we seek what is lovely, we find beauty even in difficult seasons. When we notice what is commendable, we're less prone to criticism. When we pursue excellence, we find satisfaction in doing our best. When we praise what is praiseworthy, we participate in eternal purposes.

This journey of thought transformation isn't meant to be walked alone. Throughout Scripture, we see the importance of community in supporting our spiritual growth. Share what you've learned with others. Form a small group to discuss and practice these principles together. Keep a journal of how God is changing your thought patterns. Mentor someone else in applying these truths. The impact of these eight qualities can ripple out far beyond your own life when shared in community.

Consider creating specific times and places in your daily routine for practicing each quality. Perhaps your morning commute becomes a time to notice lovely things in God's creation. Maybe your lunch break becomes an opportunity to encourage something commendable in a coworker. Your evening review might include identifying moments of truth and justice from your day. Your prayer time could focus on one virtue each week for eight weeks. Imagine the growth in your mindset that would come from that!

As you move forward from these pages, may these eight qualities become more than words you've read about—may they become the familiar paths your mind naturally travels. May they be the filter through which you process your experiences, the standard against which you measure your thoughts, and the blueprint for building a thought life that honors God and brings peace to your soul. Let them guide you in your personal devotions, your family life, your work environment, your church involvement, and your community engagement.

When I was inspired to write this book, I was a sophomore in college. Now I'm publishing it as a recent graduate, and a lot has changed since! When I started writing, I had temporarily retired from the track team. However, after going through a summer of intense reflection of my true identity, I returned to the sport my junior year. And all my health issues disappeared—praise God! I was no longer putting so much pressure on myself to perform a certain way, and my identity was now in Christ. That changed everything. I met and started dating my soon-to-be husband, AJ. I also graduated and got my first full-time job! Through all these changes, I still had one dream: I wanted to finish this book and spread these truths to people everywhere. I hope to do speaking engagements and hold workshops to keep discussing these topics. They are so important!

Whatever is true, whatever is honorable, whatever is just, whatever is pure, whatever is lovely, whatever is commendable, whatever is excellent, whatever is praiseworthy—these aren't just words on a page. They're stepping-stones on the path to a transformed mind, a peaceful heart, and a life that reflects the character of God Himself. They're the qualities that shaped the heroes of our faith, and they're the qualities God is developing in you through the power of His Spirit.

The journey doesn't end here; it begins anew each morning. With each sunrise comes a fresh opportunity to choose your thought focus, to practice these principles, and to experience the peace that comes from aligning your mind with God's truth. May you continue to think on these things, and may the God of peace be with you as you do. Remember, every thought captive to Christ is a victory, every meditation on these qualities is a step toward transformation, and every moment spent dwelling on these things is an investment in eternal value.

Now may the Lord of peace himself give you peace at all times and in every way as you continue to think on these things. May your mind be renewed, your heart be transformed, and your life be a testament to the power of God's Word lived out through intentional thought and practice.

About the Author

Madyson Ray is a multifaceted leader whose passion for spiritual growth and holistic wellness shapes both her ministry and professional life. As the director of church operations at Full Life Church in Fremont, Nebraska, she brings her unique blend of business acumen and spiritual insight to serve the local church community.

Born and raised in Nebraska, Madyson achieved the remarkable accomplishment of completing a triple major in Psychology, Sociology, and Business, reflecting her deep interest in understanding human behavior, social dynamics, and organizational leadership. This diverse academic background provides her with a distinctive lens through which she approaches biblical teaching and spiritual formation.

Beyond her role in church leadership, Madyson is dedicated to helping others achieve physical and spiritual wellness as a certified personal trainer, nutritionist, and weight management specialist. This combination of spiritual leadership and wellness coaching allows her to minister to the whole person—body, mind, and spirit.

Whatever Is marks Madyson's debut as an author, though her passion for biblical teaching and personal development has long been evident in her various professional roles. Her approach to spiritual growth is both practical and deeply rooted in Scripture, drawing from her extensive understanding of human behavior and group dynamics gained through her academic studies and professional experience.

Madyson's ministry is characterized by her ability to bridge the gap between biblical wisdom and practical application, making ancient truths accessible and relevant to contemporary women. Through her writing and teaching, she encourages women to develop a biblical mind-set that transforms every aspect of their lives.

www.ingramcontent.com/pod-product-compliance
Lightning Source LLC
Chambersburg PA
CBHW030835090426
42737CB00009B/977